A HISTORY

of

JEWISH EDUCATION

in the

SOVIET UNION

by

Elias Schulman

KTAV PUBLISHING HOUSE, INC. · NEW YORK

PHILIP W. LOWN GRADUATE CENTER
FOR CONTEMPORARY JEWISH STUDIES,
BRANDEIS UNIVERSITY.
WALTHAM, MASSACHUSETTS

THE PHILIP W. LOWN GRADUATE CENTER FOR
CONTEMPORARY JEWISH STUDIES

INSTITUTE FOR EAST EUROPEAN JEWISH STUDIES
BRANDEIS UNIVERSITY

Previously Published and Announced

1. Erich Goldhagen, editor—*Ethnic Minorities in the Soviet Union,* Frederick A. Praeger, 1968.
2. Joshua Rothenberg—*An Annotated Bibliography of Writings on Judaism Published in the Soviet Union, 1960–1965,* Brandeis University, 1969.
3. Yehoshua Gilboa—*Black Years of Soviet Jewry,* Little, Brown, 1971.
4. Elias Schulman—*A History of Jewish Education in the Soviet Union (1918–1948),* Ktav and Brandeis University, 1971.
5. Joshua Rothenberg—*The Jewish Religion in the Soviet Union,* Ktav and Brandeis University, 1971.

SBN 87068-145-1

Library of Congress Catalog Card Number: 73-138849
Manufactured in the United States of America

Table of Contents

About the Author

Elias Schulman was born in Slutsk, Byelorussia. He received his early education at the modernized Hebrew school, followed by three years at the Russian school. Arriving in the United States in 1922 he pursued his studies at the City College of New York, spent a year at the Yivo Institute for Jewish Social Studies in Vilna, and then Poland. He received his doctorate from Dropsie University, and has contributed many articles to Jewish and Anglo-Jewish journals. He is the author of *Yiddish Literature in the United States* (written in Yiddish), *Young Vilna* (Yiddish), *Studies in Soviet Yiddish Literature, Problems in Research of the History of Yiddish Literature* (in Hebrew), *Israel Tsinberg, His Life and Work*. Dr. Schulman is, at present, Librarian at the Board of Jewish Education in New York City, and is a member of the faculty of the Jewish Teachers' Seminary and People's University in the same city.

Preface

My interest in the study of Jewish life in Russia goes back three decades, to the summer of 1936, when I visited Russia to become acquainted with Jewish cultural life and the problems faced by Jews in a Communist society.

I wish to thank those who encouraged me during the years that I worked on this study, in particular the late Professor Abraham N. Neumann, President Emeritus of Dropsie University, Professor Meir Ben-Horin, and Dr. Azriel Eisenberg, formerly executive vice-president of the Jewish Education Committee.

Deserving of special thanks are Miss Dina Abramowicz, Librarian of the Yivo Institute for Jewish Research, for putting at my disposal the rich holdings of the Institute library; and Mr. Hillel Kempinsky of the Kursky Archives for letting me use the valuable material found in that collection.

I am grateful to Professor Thomas E. Bird for his suggestions and his reading of the manuscript.

E.S.

Introduction

Much has been written about the Jews in the U.S.S.R. but very little attention has been given to the Yiddish-school system whose brief existence was encouraged by a regime that was ideologically opposed to it from the outset. Most studies refer to the schools in a few brief paragraphs or pages. Salo W. Baron, in *The Russian Jew, Under Tsars and Soviets* (New York: 1964), has less than five pages on the subject; Solomon M. Schwartz, in the *Jews in the Soviet Union* (Syracuse: 1951), devotes eight pages to the Yiddish schools; there are two pages on Yiddish schools in occupied Poland written by Bernard D. Weinryb in *The Jews in Soviet Satellites* by Peter Meyer, Bernard D. Weinryb, Eugene Duschinsky, and Nicholas Sylvain (Syracuse: 1953); and Jacob Lestschinsky, in *Dos Sovetishe Yidntum,* "Soviet Jewry" (New York: 1941), provides us with a twenty-page essay. The various newspaper and magazine articles are generally not scholarly and shed little light on the subject, with the exception of Weinryb's essay "Das jüdische Schulwesen in Sowjetrussland" in *Monatsschrift für Geschichte und Wissenschaft des Judentums* (1931), pp. 455–462.

This study is the result of exhaustive research on a school system whose rise, development, and decline is not only indicative of the shifts in the Soviet Jewish policy, but is an accurate barometer of the climate within Russia's Jewish community of close to three million. Original source material, such as reports, memoirs, decrees, statements, and other documents which appeared in Soviet publications, has been used almost exclusively. Curricula, textbooks, and school catalogues were also examined, and articles by Soviet writers about the Yiddish schools were critically evaluated. In addition to data concerning the establishment of the schools, their operation and demise, the causes underlying the difficulties which these ill-fated schools encountered are analyzed.

Neither Lenin nor Stalin recognized the Jews as an ethnic or even as a religious group. In a series of articles that Lenin wrote in 1903, he expressed the belief that Jews constituted a caste which tended to assimilate with the general population under liberal Western governments. Under a new revolutionary regime the Russian Jews would be given the opportunity to assimilate, thereby solving the Jewish question. In *Marxism and the National Colonial Problem,* published in 1913, Stalin supported this idea and caustically suggested that the complete assimilation of the Jews be part of Communist policy.

Despite this principle, the new Communist dictatorship of 1917 faced realities, including the need for supporters. The government eventually recognized the Jewish nationality, unofficially, and saw its culture as worthy of development, although this about-face was obviously an expedient. There were many Jews among the important leaders of the new regime and many of the rank-and-file Communists had come from the Jewish labor movement, which included ex-Bundists, Labor Zionists and Socialist Territorialists. Jews were classed with other national groups in the U.S.S.R. and were encouraged to establish a Yiddish-school system.

Jewish Communists hastened to take advantage of the official sanction. They organized, as part of the Soviet school system, Yiddish schools which were in fact only national in form, but completely Communist in content. Yiddish was the language of instruction in a curriculum which included Yiddish literature; but Jewish history was taught with a Marxist interpretation, and Communist propaganda pervaded all aspects of the school program. Jewishness, in the form of nationalism, tradition, and Jewish values, was assiduously avoided, and even the Hebrew component of Yiddish was modified or eliminated.

The leaders of these schools used their official status to compel the enrollment of Jewish children. Those Jewish parents who identified with the Jewish people lacked enthusiasm for schools which eliminated tradition, Hebrew, and Jewish nationalism; those who wished to assimilate and lose their Jewish identity wanted nothing to do with a school which was Jewish, even though only in name. Despite this, in the early thirties about 50% of all the Jewish children in Belorussia and 60% of the Jewish children in the Ukraine attended Yiddish schools.

The proponents of the schools claimed that these were the first Jewish secular schools designed to meet the requirements of Jews in a modern world. These false claims won no new supporters. Jewish secular schools had been in existence since the beginning of the century under the auspices of the Jewish Labor Bund, Labor Zionists, Folkists (Populists) and various democratic groups. In a number of areas in Russia, during World War I, such schools had emerged and served as models for the Soviet Yiddish schools. Along with the Hebrew secular Tarbut schools* and Jewish schools in the Russian language they were taken over by the new school system, purged of their Jewishness, and proclaimed as the optimum in modern Jewish education.

The new schools were plagued by serious problems from the start. They faced ideological hostility and, at best, an apathetic clientele. Their effectiveness in developing Jewish attitudes and transmitting Jewish knowledge was slight. Nevertheless, the Jewish children who attended these schools were closer to the Jewish people than those who did not.

This is a study of these problems, as well as their ramifications. An attempt has been made to include and evaluate all aspects of the Soviet Yiddish-school systems, and it is hoped that this will rectify many misconceptions about the schools as well as shed some light on the fate of Jews in a Communist society.

*These were elementary and secondary schools, where the language of instruction was Hebrew and the philosophy was Zionism.

CHAPTER 1

The Theoretical Base for
the Secular Yiddish Schools

THE Soviet Yiddish-school system, which existed between the years 1918 and 1948, was descended from the secular Yiddish schools which originated in Russia at the beginning of the twentieth century. Schools for Jewish children of the same type were established in September 1939, in the newly occupied territories of western Belorussia and the western Ukraine, and functioned until June 1941, when the Nazis occupied the territories.

The Tsarist government had prohibited the establishment of secular schools which operated in the native language. After the Revolution of 1905, some minority nationalities were permitted to establish their own schools although this right was denied the Jews. Even in 1914, after the Duma passed a law giving such rights to all nationalities, the Jews were not granted this privilege.[1] Despite the generally negative Tsarist attitude towards Yiddish schools, a few were opened at the beginning of the twentieth century, and the instruction of Yiddish, and in Yiddish, was introduced into some Jewish schools in Russia.

The rise of nationalism in Eastern Europe, the awakening of oppressed nationalities, their demands for national recognition and for recognition of their languages influenced the Jewish masses.

1

The rise of the Jewish revolutionary and labor movements, the founding of the Jewish Socialist Labor Bund in 1897, and the development of Folkism,[2] gave impetus to the demands for a secular Jewish school to be taught in Yiddish, the language of the Jewish people in the Russian Empire.

According to the census of 1897, ninety-seven percent of the Jewish population in the Tsarist Empire gave Yiddish as their mother tongue. Even after the inroads of assimilation, and after Poland and Lithuania, birthplace of the least assimilated Jews, were no longer part of the Soviet Union, the census of 1926 showed that 72.6 percent of the Jews in the Soviet Union gave Yiddish as their mother tongue. The percentage in Belorussia was 90.7, in the Ukraine 76.1, and in Central Russia 50.3.[3]

At the turn of the century the old-fashioned *ḥeder*,[4] the dominating Jewish school, was outdated and the time was propitious for the establishment of secular schools for Jewish children. Peter Marek (1862–1920), the historian of Jewish education in Russia in the nineteenth century, concluded his study with the following statement:

> Jewish education is not only a system for the religious but strives to take its place in the secular hierarchy of knowledge. Language, Literature, History, carry on a successful struggle for primacy with religion. Ritual values are replaced by national values, which made the first break in the almost unbreakable fortress of the Heder. Taking into consideration new views and new problems of Jewish education, the "heder *melamdim*" were forced, in one way or another, to bring into the program of religious education some secular correlatives. Various textbooks on grammar and even history began to penetrate into many of the Hadorim. To be sure many of the teachers *(melamdim)* guided themselves by an instinct for self-preservation, but found it too difficult to adapt themselves to the new path. However, the mere fact of the search for new paths, signified that the teachers themselves saw the Heder in need of reforms. Simultaneously with this recognition, many new model Hadorim developed in many communities, which completely divorced themselves from the old, narrow, religious tradition. These new schools brought into the teaching of Jewish subjects a secular character and pure pedagogic methods. The Heder problem, which for so long defied a solution, entered a more favorable phase.
>
> This trend to secularism was the main path followed by Jewish education in the last period.[5]

A study of Jewish education in Russia showed that in 1894 there were 13,689 ḥadorim, with 17,740 *melamdim* (teachers), and 201,964 pupils. In 1898, a study showed that in twenty-five guberniyas ("provinces") of the pale of settlement which included Poland, with a Jewish population of 1,420,653, there were 7,248 ḥadorim with 202,956 pupils.[6] This meant that there was one ḥeder for every group of twenty-eight children of school age, and that 53.8 percent of Jewish children of school age attended a ḥeder.[7]

Besides the old-fashioned ḥadorim, there were a number of Jewish secular schools conducted in the Russian language. In 1899 there were 820 Jewish schools which were private, community, and government schools and whose pupils exceeded fifty thousand.[8] These schools were Jewish in the sense that the pupils and some of the teachers were Jewish, but the language of instruction was Russian. The Jewish content of these schools was very slight, amounting to some elements of Jewish religion and some parts of the Bible taught in Russian translation.

According to an estimate by a well-known educator, Ch. Fialkov (1873–1920), there were, in 1910, 325,000 pupils in the ḥadorim, while 474,000 children of school age did not attend any school at all.[9] According to a report of the Ministry of Education there were, in 1912, 7,743 ḥadorim, 773 secular schools, and 147 community *Talmud Torahs*.[10]

The Talmud Torahs were community schools organized for the children of the poor, where no tuition fee was charged. Special permits were required for organizing these schools, in which secular subjects were taught, whose charters required that Russian should be the language of instruction. Jewish subjects, such as Bible, were permitted to be taught in Yiddish. The Talmud Torah differed from the ḥadorim by introducing secular, nonreligious subjects.[11]

By the end of the nineteenth century a new school appeared, the *Heder Metukan,* the reformed Hebrew school. The Ḥeder Metukan employed Hebrew as the language of instruction, and taught Hebrew language, literature, Jewish history, and sometimes held classes in the geography of Eretz Israel (Palestine). The Bible was a major subject. The school was a direct development of the Zionist movement and the movement for the revival of the Hebrew language.

The Heder Metukan differed from the old heder in both content and form. The pupils were divided into classes during a school day which ended at about three or four o'clock in the afternoon. The natural teaching method of *Ivrit b'Ivrit* (i.e., Hebrew taught in Hebrew, the Direct Method) was employed, making the atmosphere less religious and more modern than in the old-fashioned heder. The spirit of the school was Zionist and Hebraist.[12]

But the Heder Metukan could not satisfy the demands of the times. Most, although not all, of these schools ignored such general subjects as Russian, arithmetic, and general history. The religious elements were dissatisfied with its modernism, and the Jewish middle class that strove to give its children a general education lost interest in a school which limited its curriculum to Hebrew, Hebrew literature, and the Bible.[13]

The Heder Metukan was popular for a time but it did not take the place of the old heder. Zevi Scharfstein, in his *History of Jewish Education,* states that "the founding of the Hadorim Metukanim spread rapidly, until there was not a city or town in the pale of settlement, where such a school was not established."[14] Naturally, this was an exaggeration, for in 1912, in the Yekaterinoslav guberniya or province, there were ninety-five Hadorim, and not a single Heder Metukan. In the guberniya of Volynia there were 108 Hadorim and not one Heder Metukan.[15] The Heder Metukan never became the Jewish public school, nevertheless it did manage to exist until the revolutionary period in 1917–1918, when it developed into the secular Tarbut schools. Those parents who were ready to send their children to a modern school preferred the secular Russian school and the democratic elements introduced the idea of a normal school for Jewish children to be taught in Yiddish.

At the beginning of the twentieth century, the socialist and various Labor and Folkist groups and parties formulated programs for a modern Jewish school where a curriculum taught in Yiddish should include both Jewish and general subjects. The majority of the Jewish educators agreed that great reforms were necessary in Jewish education to meet the demands of the times. Three distinct groups appeared: the assimilators who wanted a school with Russian as the language of instruction; the Zionists who worked for a school with Hebrew as the language of instruction; and the various groups of socialists, Folkists, and Yiddishists, who thought the time was ripe for a folk school with Yiddish as the language of instruction. We will discuss here the theoretical works of those who evolved the idea of the secular Yiddish school in Russia, from which further developed the Yiddish-school system.

Joseph Becker published a series of articles in 1906[16] in which he discussed the position of Yiddish in the Jewish school. He felt that Yiddish, not Hebrew, was the mother tongue of the Jewish child, and that the principle of the use of the mother tongue in the public school could be applied to Yiddish only. The author concluded his series by stating that "the child can develop normally only when it gets its education in its mother tongue. The public school cannot be [conducted] in anything but the native language." Becker quotes a line by a poet from Provence that, "blessed is the delicate word that sounds near the cradle." "In the words that sounded near our cradle lies the hope in education for the people."

Boris Levinson, a graduate of the Vilna Jewish Teachers' Institute[17] and a director of a community Talmud Torah in the Crimea, published an essay, "Di Yidishe Folkshul" (The Jewish Folk Shul)[18] which promoted the use of Yiddish for instruction in the Jewish school. Levinson discussed the nature and the shortcomings of the Ḥeder, the Ḥeder Metukan, the community Talmud Torahs, and the state Jewish schools. He believed that the Ḥeder Metukan failed because it concentrated on Hebrew and did not include general subjects in its curriculum. He compared it to those schools that concentrated on teaching Latin and Greek grammar and ignored the best works of Latin and Greek literature.

In the State Russian Language Schools for Jewish children, the students were really taught by government functionaries whose aim was to Russify the children. The school and its teachers remained strangers to the Jewish population, although the schools had been in existence a long time. The Jewish subjects that were in the curriculum, Levinson calls "merely a comedy."

The author mentioned that in some community Talmud Torahs teachers successfully introduced the study of Yiddish, to which the pupils reacted with studious enthusiasm. Yiddish was introduced because, "life demands it. The pupils will have to know how to read a Yiddish paper, will have to know how to write letters in Yiddish—and if the Talmud Torah will not teach it to them, the poor parents will have to hire private teachers to teach them how to read and write Yiddish."

In a second essay, "Vegn Natsionaler Dertsiung"[19] (About National Education), Levinson formulated the objectives of Jewish education. He suggested that in the Jewish school, Jewish culture and Jewish customs should be taught, and he criticized the socialist Jewish intelligentsia for neglecting Jewish customs:

> Our intelligentsia and our workers remove all colors from their living patterns, everything is gray and colorless. I do not see any sin against progress when a clean cloth covers the table on the Sabbath, when we light candles on a Friday night, or when, during the Passover, the holiday of spring and freedom, our homes are brightened, or when we fill our homes with greenery on Shavouot—or when national mourning is felt on the 9th of Ab.

Boris Levinson concluded that the aim of the new Jewish intelligentsia should be to build a new secular Jewish school,

> to create a Yiddish literature that should embrace all sciences, popularize the whole Jewish history, to publish original and translated works that mirror Jewish life, both contemporary and the old, to translate all classical works of world literature, to collect folk songs and melodies, folk tales—this is a program not for one year—but this must become the aim of our community. To accomplish this work, we must begin right now.

Another writer of that period who wrote a great deal about Jewish educational problems was Maria Yakovlevna Frumkin, who wrote under the name "Esther."[20] She expressed the socialist approach to Jewish education:

> The Jewish worker created national values, and a national culture, without making it a special objective, and the education that he will provide for his children will also be national, although that will not be the primary objective. The reason is that the Jewish worker is deeply national.[21]

In the same essay Maria Frumkin suggested that the Jewish workers demand that Yiddish be taught in the community Talmud Torahs, and in both the private and community Russian-language Jewish schools. The Jewish workers would have the support of some of the progressive Jewish teachers "who feel that their work in a foreign-language school is useless," of whom a few had introduced Yiddish clandestinely.

In another article, Maria Frumkin writes in favor of Yiddish:

> The language of instruction in each school must be the mother tongue of the children—for each nationality there must be established separate schools and the national schools should be in the language of the nationalities. Until the time when national-cultural centers will be established, each national group in each town and county must organize a school council. This council should be elected in secret, equal and direct elections. The demand should also be made that among the various languages that will be used as languages of instruction, Yiddish must be recognized.[22]

In addition to essays, Maria Frumkin published a book entitled *On the Question of the Jewish Folk School.*[23] She begins her study by stating that:

> There is evidence of a new Jewish public opinion that is developing. I do not exaggerate the value of these symptoms. Long is the road that Yiddish has to travel before it will be recognized. But the historical process goes on. The Jewish workers have a great task— to get rid of the obstructionists (p. 4).

Frumkin pointed out that the awakening of the oppressed nationalities had put in the forefront the demands for a national public school, in the mother tongue. This kind of school was to be the "Aleph Bet"[24] of the national life. Such cultured nations as the Germans, the Polish people in Russia, and the Czechs and other minorities in Austria were struggling for school systems in their native languages, as were also such poor people with a primitive culture as the Yakuts.

The Jews did not even have the freedom to build their own schools, as Frumkin writes:

> On the Jewish street, which is rich with national castles in the air, and poor with positive daily national work, the idea of a school in its own language is little felt and little known. Only the class-conscious proletariat feels the necessity, and sympathy for such a school is expressed by small groups of the nationally conscious intelligentsia.

Frumkin then continues:

> It is natural that the broad Jewish masses, the most oppressed of all the oppressed, have not arrived yet at a state where they can appreciate their own language, and to comprehend that in one's own

tongue one can acquire an education. It is natural that they do not devote themselves to pedagogic problems, and do not realize yet, that only in one's mother tongue can their child acquire an education (pp. 5 ff.).

Even those groups who believed in Yiddish as a language and as a culture, advocated Russian as the language of instruction in the Jewish folk school. They reasoned that, since the Jews constituted a minority, they should know the language of the majority. They admitted that education in the mother tongue would be easier, but declared that the children who acquire the Russian language will have the rich Russian culture opened to them.

Frumkin defined the aim of education as the development of the spiritual and moral tendencies in man. Because the educated worker was more class conscious, popular education of workers and children was the best means available in the struggle for a better future. Schools were a continuation of both the home and the street, where the new knowledge the child acquired was interwoven with that received at home and in his neighborhood. Everything a child brought to school was expressed in the mother tongue, and each word lived for the child as a symbol of group solidarity and consciousness (p. 9). When the teacher read a poem, he would point out the different words and the function that the words played. But the children would understand the meaning of the poem only when the language was familiar to them. The child could memorize the poem, but it would have no meaning for him. To strengthen her position, Frumkin quoted from the Vienna *Arbeiterzeitung* of October 1909, that children in Slovakia failed in their examinations because the instructions and the examinations were given to them in a foreign language.

The visual method, stated Frumkin, depended not on the textbook or the teacher, but on what the child saw. Pictures and experimentation are the basis for this method. Modern pedagogy is concerned with the child's participation where success depends upon his actions. All actions are fused and coordinated through words. Without mastery of language, the child cannot coordinate all his actions and would not be able to comprehend and learn (pp. 17 and 18). A Jewish child who reads Russian poetry will not understand it well, and will forget both the language and the poetry a few years after graduating.

Frumkin believed that a language possessed a spirit and a soul. Each nation contributed of its own self to its language. Each word has an inner meaning which is sometimes different or impossible to translate. The hidden meanings form the poetry, the mystique and the quiet tones are the elements that make up the national poetry. In order to get at the hidden meaning of Peretz or Einhorn, the language must be part of one's self. A Russian child, if he received instruction in Yiddish, would never fully appreciate such lines as David Einhorn's:

> Ruik, ruik, shoklt ir geloktes grinem kepl
> Main vaisinke beriozkele un davnt on a shir;
> Zay shoin beriozkele mispalel oych far mir.

> (Quietly, quietly shakes its curly green head
> My white birch tree and prays without end;
> Pray for me too my birch tree.)

A Christian child who attended a church would not understand Einhorn's image of how the birch tree shakes and prays, while a Jewish child would understand it without difficulty. But the mother tongue is not the only key to the newspaper, the book, and knowledge, and to, it must be added, the literary language (p. 22).

Political, economic, technological, and literary terminology which cannot be acquired at home must be learned in school where children would learn the official language of the country. In order to understand a country's literature, one must be acquainted with its atmosphere, period, and history, and this is learned in school— but a foreign-language elementary school deprives the child of its own history and literature (p. 23).

Mme. Frumkin insists that:

> In the name of their most vital interest, in the name of their long-suffering children, who lose the best part of their youth, Jewish parents must demand an elementary school in their native language. In the name of scientific pedagogy all honest Jewish teachers must protest against becoming tools in damaging the new generation.

Then the author introduces the idea of socialism:

> In the name of its class struggle, the Jewish proletariat must, with all its energy, demand a folk school that should permit its children to have an open door to education and culture—a folk school in the mother tongue (p. 24).

Mme. Frumkin pointed out that emigration plays a big part in Jewish life, and the few years of schooling should be utilized in preparing the child for life, in helping him to adjust to the outside community:

> The language of instruction should be one's native language. The foreign language should and could be only one subject of study. This is the demand of the cultural interests of the Jewish masses. These are also the demands of their economic interests (p. 31).

Mme. Frumkin analyzed, and dismissed as ignorant talk, the arguments that Yiddish is not a language, that it has no grammar, that it does not "sound right" (p. 37). She also traced the development of Yiddish, including its dialects, pointing out that most living languages are spoken differently in various localities, that "no one will dare say that Russian is a corrupted language because it is derived from old Slavonic" (p. 40). Yiddish spelling, Frumkin points out, has a good deal of variety, as have all languages, but eventually a unified way of spelling will be introduced. The same varieties existed in Russian spelling until the grammar and spellings were standardized by the government (p. 48). The question as to whether a language is "beautiful" or "ugly" is totally unscientific (p. 49).

The idea of a Yiddish folk school which expressed the cultural, political, and economic interests of the Jewish masses, was not sufficiently popular with the people, as Frumkin pointed out. The Zionists and Hebraists were against it, and the Jewish masses who were influenced by them were not conscious of the necessity for the Yiddish school (p. 54). But Mme. Frumkin felt that this indifference could be overcome by the national renaissance which was taking place in the Jewish community (p. 55). Many other nationalities, not only the Jews, were ashamed of their own language; but when the masses awoke, due to economic and political changes, they would demand recognition for their own tongue (p. 56). Such a process of awakening could already be observed in Austria, where the Czechs, Slovaks, and Ruthenians were taking greater pride in their folk heritage. The paradox was that the bourgeoisie, which formerly imitated the ruling nation and adopted the reigning language, became the most nationalist; but only the proletariat finds the middle way (p. 58).

Mme. Frumkin stated that it became difficult for the assimilated intellectual to find a place for himself in the "foreign" field. The reigning nation demanded complete and absolute submission, but such complete and total assimilation was impossible. Therefore the national intelligentsia and the middle class were forced to fight for their own language. The intelligentsia then would be forced to create an atmosphere where it would be able to utilize its intellectual labor (p. 61). When Polish was recognized in Galicia, it created a field for Polish intellectuals who, until then, had no possibility of making use of their language and culture (p. 62).

As the masses became more cultured, they would have a greater need for the services of professionals. In the free competitive market, the doctor, the lawyer, and the dentist who spoke the language of the people had a better chance of surviving and prospering than the one who did not. When competition was slight, even a photographer did not speak to his client in his native tongue. But things were different now (p. 65). A folkist intelligentsia was emerging from the Yeshivas who received their education outside the school (externs). It was true that, due to the strengthening of the reaction, the cultural development was slowed down, but it had not been stopped.

The fight for the recognition of the Jewish nationality, declared Frumkin, would also enhance the fight for the recognition of Yiddish and the Yiddish school. The Jewish middle class, whose members produced the teachers, would be forced to fight for a Jewish school which would be secular, democratic, free, and compulsory. It would be at least an eight-year school so that those who were to continue would be able to enter the fifth year of the gymnasiums (gimnazia).[25] The schools would have parents' organizations which should have a voice in the school administration. Mme. Frumkin repeats that the schools should be administered by the organs of the national autonomy which should be recognized by the government.

To Mme. Frumkin, a really democratic school could not exist in a capitalist society where there was so much suffering (p. 75). The national, democratic folk school was not an end in itself for the proletariat, it was only a tool to make easier its struggle for the future (p. 75). She laid the basis for the new Jewish school—Yiddish, secular, democratic, and socialist—thus formulating the Bundist program of Jewish education.

The eighth conference of the Bund that was held in Lemberg in 1910 adopted a resolution which stated:

> Until the national cultural autonomy will be established and re-organized, which transfers the schools to the jurisdiction of the nationalities, the struggle must be carried on that schools for each nationality should be established and that the language of instruction should be in the mother tongue. All limitations on using the mother tongue in government institutions, in public meetings, in the press and in the private and community schools should be abolished.[26]

The Socialist Territorialists and the Sejmists[27] also demanded the establishment of Jewish Folk Schools using the Yiddish language. While the Sejmists believed in a Jewish school conducted by the organs of the national personal autonomy, the Territorialists advocated the establishment of school associations, which should build and supervise the schools.[28]

In August 1908, the conference for the Yiddish language was held in Czernowitz, Bukovina, at that time in Austria. The leading people of the conference were Yitzhok Leib Peretz, Nathan Birnbaum, Chaim Zhitlowsky, Sholem Asch, Abraham Reisen, Hirsh David Nomberg, and Mme. Maria Frumkin. This was a non-Party conference where various intellectuals assembled to discuss the problem of Yiddish and Yiddish culture.

Peretz, in his address, said:

> We tell the world, we are a Jewish nation and Yiddish is our language. We want to live with Yiddish and with it create our values, and we don't intend to give away those rights. We don't want to serve others. Valets cannot create cultural values. We do not want to be atomized and offer our creations to the various states. One nation, Jews, its language is Yiddish, and in this language we strive to gather together our culture, to create our culture, to stir our souls, and culturally to reunite with all the people.[29]

The conference adopted this resolution:

> The first conference of the Yiddish language recognizes Yiddish as a national language of the Jewish people and demands its political, social, and cultural equality. The conference finds it necessary to declare that each participant in the conference, and also all future members of the organization, have the freedom to maintain their attitude to Hebrew according to their personal convictions.[30]

But not only the socialist and revolutionary intelligentsia agitated for Yiddish and Yiddish schools. The Czernowitz Conference represented those intellectuals who espoused the new secularist, Yiddishist trends. The monthly journal, *Di Yidishe Velt,* which was edited by Samuel Niger, became the organ of the nonpolitical Yiddishists.

When a new Russian imperial census was planned, *Di Yidishe Velt* published an article by its editor which said:

> It is necessary to propagandize that the Jews should claim Yiddish as their mother tongue. This is important not only for tactical purposes but from the point of view of principle. It is necessary to implant in the Jewish population a conscious, not only instinctive, love for one's own language. It is important that everyone should understand that the mother tongue is something precious not only for the individual but for the entire community. We must not tire of repeating that the fact that 97% of the Jews in Russia speak and understand Yiddish is not only a fact that must be utilized, because there is no other choice, but it is a great factor in the cultural and political life of the Jewish people. We must state it with pride and joy, not with hidden regret. We must prepare to proclaim Yiddish as our language in the forthcoming national census.[31]

The journal also discussed the new law (passed by the Duma in 1914) governing schools. It permitted the introduction of the native language of the children in private schools. S. Niger pointed out that this law should be utilized by the Jewish schools, and Yiddish should be introduced into the private Jewish schools.[32]

S. Niger quoted a Jewish teacher who stated, "the soul of the Jewish child cannot be opened to its full width, because of the foreign language that is being used as the language of instruction." The author also compared the writing of Jewish children both in Yiddish and Russian and pointed out that these writings constitute the best arguments against the use of Russian and for the use of Yiddish in the Jewish schools.[33]

In connection with the all-Russian conference for popular education, the same journal published an article which again took up the problem of the Jewish school. Says the writer, Samuel Charney (S. Niger):

> We know what a bitter and sorrowful part the Russian school plays in the regions that have a non-Russian population. We all know that it is not a Russian but a Russification school. The chil-

dren that study there speak, at home and in the street, not Russian, but Ukrainian, Belorussian, Latvian, and Yiddish. But in the schools these languages cannot be mentioned. In the school the children must break their teeth on a language that they do not know and with which they cannot be as intimate as with their own mother tongue. In the school they must not only study the foreign language (no one is against studying the Russian language) but they must study in the foreign language all subjects, even the history and religion of their own people. From a purely pedagogical point of view such a school cannot satisfy anyone.[34]

The same writer stated in another essay that:

Most Jewish children, as is well known, are outside a normal Folk School.[35] We must, at least, create a children's literature where the pupils of the assimilatory school would receive the essential national education and, for the thousands of those children that remain outside the school, we should prepare a literature which would enable them to get some elementary knowledge, and thus help them to develop. By creating this type of literature, the future reader is being prepared for the Yiddish press, and for both the scientific book and the belles lettres.[36]

Not only Jewish socialists and unaffiliated intellectuals saw the necessity for a secular Jewish school with Yiddish as the language of instruction, but even some Zionists. It is true that the Zionist movement favored Hebrew for the Heder Metukan and for a secular Jewish school where Hebrew would be the language of instruction; but one active Zionist writer realized the importance of Yiddish in the Jewish school. This writer was Dr. Joseph Lurie (1871–1937). In a series of articles which he published in the Yiddish daily, *Der Fraynd,* in 1905–1906 he stated:

Into Yiddish the Jews have put a part of their soul, and that is the reason that the people consider it their language, love it, and feel insulted when the intelligentsia, both the real and the false, is ashamed of it and avoids it—Yiddish is the language of the heder— which is our public school, and must remain the language of conversation and study in the future improved Jewish Folk School and in all private Jewish schools. Yiddish must be not only the medium of communication between teachers and pupils, but also the language of instruction of all subjects, as arithmetic, geography, history, biology. The Folk School with the folk language is the foundation of national education. On this foundation the school must be built. In the secondary schools, for Jewish children, Yiddish also has to be the language of instruction. The Jews in Russia can have many Jewish *Gimnazias, Realschulen* and Commercial High Schools, and we can attain them, if we will adopt the principle that our folk language is Yiddish and that in this language Jewish education must be conducted. This is not a dream, nor is it a wild demand. This demand is in our national interests, and the existence of our nation calls for it.[37]

The beginning of the twentieth century marked the period where the idea of a Jewish secular school, with Yiddish as the language of instruction, matured. The struggle of the various nationalities, both in Russia and neighboring Austro-Hungary, for the right to their own languages, encouraged the Jews to conduct a similar struggle. The theoreticians of the Jewish political parties as well as nonaffiliated intellectuals laid the ideological foundation for such a school. The old-fashioned heder, with its limited curriculum of the Bible and Talmud, could no longer satisfy the demands of the times. The first secular Yiddish school was established without governmental permission. Yiddish was also introduced clandestinely in a number of private Russian-language Jewish schools and in some community Talmud Torahs. The Tsarist empire could not completely prevent the emergence of the Yiddish schools.

NOTES

1. Abraham Golomb, "Di Yidishe Veltlekhe Shul" (The Yiddish Secular School) in *Shul Almanakh* (School Almanac), Philadelphia, 1935, pp. 20–21.
2. A movement in Russia which emerged at the end of the nineteenth century. It was based on the belief that the majority of Jews would remain in the countries in which they lived, and that they were entitled to civil rights and cultural autonomy. The establishment of secular Jewish schools was a major plank in their platform.
3. Solomon M. Schwartz, *The Jews in the Soviet Union*, Syracuse Press, 1951, p. 131. Y. Paykin, in his analysis of the census of 1926 in Belorussia, showed that while 18% of Belorussian and 63% of Polish people gave Russian as their mother tongue, less than 10% of Jews gave languages other than Yiddish as their mother tongue. Paykin also shows that 3,930 people declared their nationality to be Russian, but gave Yiddish as their mother tongue. Paykin thinks that these people are mostly Jews. Y. Paykin, "Some Conclusions of the Demographic Census of 1926," in *Tsaitshrift*, Vol. IV, published by the Jewish Sector of the Belorussian Academy of Science, Minsk, 1930, pp. 172–174.
4. Classically *heder* was a one-room, one-teacher, religious school.
5. Peter S. Marek, *Ocherki po istorii prosveshcheniia Evreev v Rossi* (Studies of

the History of Jewish Enlightenment in Russia), published by the Society for the Diffusion of Education among Jews, Moscow, 1909.

6. Zevi Scharfstein, *Ha-Heder be-Hayye Amenu* (The Heder in the Life of Our People) (New York, 1943); Yekhiel Shtern, *Heder un Beys-Medresh* (Heder and Beys-Medresh), New York, 1950.

7. Ch. S. Kazhdan, *Fun Heder un Shkoles tsu Tsisho* (From Heder and Schools to Tsisho), Mexico City, 1956, p. 135.

8. *Ibid.*, p. 205.

9. *Vestnik Ope*, February 1914, quoted by Kazhdan, *op. cit.*, p. 138.

10. Kazhdan, *op. cit.*, p. 138. Zevi Scharfstein gives the total of 181,944 for all enrolled Jewish children in the various schools in 1910. This figure seems to be incorrect. Zevi Scharfstein also quotes from the same report by Fialkov— but he quotes from page 76 and ignores the material on page 77. The number quoted on page 76 is an estimate by the Ministry of Education. This number applies to pupils who attended the *hadorim* which were registered by the government and where the *melamdim* had a "patent." The number given on page 77, namely 325,000, is the number given by the Statistical Bureau of the Jewish Colonization Association, and this number includes the pupils from both the registered and nonregistered *hadorim*. Here is what Fialkov writes: "Cherez Khedera ezhegodno prokhodit ne menee 325,000 detei" (p. 77). (Every year 325,000 children go through the heder.) Fialkov, "Polozhenie evreiskavo narodnovo obrazovania" ("The Condition of Jewish Public Education"), *Vestnik Ope*, (Feb. 1914), p. 77. The Russian *Evreiskaia Entsiklopediya*, Volume XV, column 593 (St. Petersburg, 1910), states that the number of children who attended *hadorim* at that time was 343,000. Scharfstein's figures, which he gives in *Toledot ha-Hinnukh be-Yisroel*, Volume I (New York, 1945), p. 394, namely, 181,949, and which he repeats in the new edition of 1960, p. 419, is therefore not the correct figure. See also: Y. Kantor, *Di Kultur Revolutsie in der Yidisher Svive*, "The Cultural Revolution in the Jewish Milieu" *(Ratn-Bildung* No. 4, May 1928, Kharkov), pp. 7–14, where he states that, in all, only 37% of the Jewish children received any form of education before the November Revolution of 1917 (p. 9).

11. Kazhdan, *op. cit.*, pp. 194–196.

12. Zevi Scharfstein, *Toledot ha-Hinnukh be-Yisroel be-Dorot ha-Achronim* (History of Jewish Education in Modern Times), Vol. I, New York, 1945, pp. 363 ff.

13. *Ibid.*, pp. 382–383. See also: Judah Pilch, *The Heder Methukan,* unpublished dissertation, Dropsie College, 1952. For curriculum see p. 94.

14. *Ibid.*, p. 377.

15. Kazhdan, *op. cit.*, p. 316.

16. "Folksshprakhn un Folksshuln" (Folk Languages and Public Schools) in *Folkstsaitung*, Nos. 18, 21, 24, 27, Vilna, March 1906.

17. This Institute trained teachers for the Russian-language Jewish schools. The graduates were mostly assimilated, and they were the carriers of assimilation among the Jews. However, some of the students later became teachers in the Hebrew and Yiddish schools.

18. *Di Naye Tsait*, No. 1, Vilna, 1908.

19. *Tsait Fragn*, No. 2, Vilna, March 1910.

20. Maria Yakovlevna Frumkin was born in 1880. She was an active Bundist, but in 1919 became a Communist and was active as a political functionary,

writer and translator of Lenin's works into Yiddish. She was "liquidated" in 1938 for Jewish nationalism and Bundism.

21. "Einike Bamerkungen Vegn Natsionaler Dertsiung" (A Few Remarks About National Education), *Tsait Fragn*, Vol. 1, Vilna, 1909.

22. "Vegn Natsionaler Dertsiung" (About National Education), *Tsait Fragn*, Vol. 5, Vilna, 1911.

23. *Tsu der Frage fun der Yidisher Folkshul* (On the Question of the Yiddish Folk School), Velt Publishers, Vilna, 1910. The book was published in three editions, the third appearing in Petrograd in 1917. The present writer used the Petrograd edition, which did not differ from the previous editions.

24. Literally, the alphabet; here, the language of the people.

25. In Russia the *gimnazia* was a classical high school.

26. Kazhdan, *op. cit.*, p. 281.

27. The Sejmists: the full name was Jewish Socialist Labor Party. It believed in an officially recognized Jewish *Sejm* (parliament) that should be the organ of the Jewish national autonomy. Politically it was affiliated with the Russian Socialist Revolutionary party.

28. "We demand that the Jewish public education should be in the hands of Jewish people, in the form of free school associations that the Jewish political groups will organize." "Our Aims," *Der Nayer Weg* (The New Road), Vilna, 1906, No. 1, Column 8 (no other date given).

29. *Di Ershte Yidishe Shprakh Konferentz, 1908* (The First Yiddish Language Conference, 1908), Library of the Yiddish Scientific Institute, Vilna, 1931, p. 76.

30. *Ibid.*, p. 107.

31. *Di Yidishe Velt*, No. 10, October 1913, Vilna, pp. 133–134. The census was not taken, as it was scheduled for 1914. The outbreak of World War I canceled it.

32. *Di Yidishe Velt*, Vol. I, No. 1, Vilna, 1913.

33. *Di Yidishe Velt*, No. 10, October 1913, p. 140.

34. *Ibid.*, No. 11, November 1913, p. 145.

35. A Folk School in this context meant a secular, elementary school.

36. *Di Yidishe Velt*, No. 5, May 1913.

37. Kazhdan, *op. cit.*, pp. 246–248.

CHAPTER 2

The First Yiddish
Secular Schools

T HE first secular Yiddish school was organized in Mir, a town in the province of Minsk, in 1898. Noah Mishkowsky, its founder, was a young man acquainted with the idea of Jewish nationalism. He believed in the idea, current at that time, that the folk language should be cultivated as a national language and as a vehicle for educating the people. Because the Yiddish language was spoken and understood by nearly all the Jews in Russia, Mishkowsky believed that it was natural that it should be utilized as the language of instruction.

Mishkowsky's home town, Mir, was the seat of the famous Mirer Yeshiva. There were numerous hadorim where Jewish boys obtained their education. As a progressive and a radical, a believer in education for the people, Mishkowsky felt it was his duty to open a secular school in the midst of the yeshiva town. He invited a few young people to act as teachers. These teachers, who originally thought that Russian should be the language of instruction, were soon won over to his point of view. Together, they worked out a curriculum patterned after the Russian elementary school, consisting of the study of the Russian language, arithmetic, geography, and Jewish history. The spirit of the school was non-

18

religious (secular), and progressive. The great difficulty was the lack of Yiddish textbooks; but the determined teachers used Russian textbooks as models from which they prepared their daily lessons.

The pupils, recruited from the poorest section of the community, were not charged for tuition. All together, in one large sparsely furnished room, the children received instruction from nine in the morning until three in the afternoon. The relationship between the children and the teachers was excellent. After nine months of teaching, the results showed that the children mastered the subjects taught in Yiddish—Jewish history, literature, geography—better than those taught in Russian—Russian history and Russian.

Mishkowsky stated:

> Then I understood that from the practical point of view, Jewish children should receive their elementary education in Yiddish. It became clear to me that our language is similar to other languages and that everything can be taught in it. At that time the prevailing opinion was that Russian and Hebrew should be the languages of instruction. Nobody dreamed about utilizing Yiddish in the modern school, although Yiddish was the language of instruction in the hadorim.[1]

Since the school had no charter and could not get one from the local government, it ceased to exist after nine months.

Mishkowsky organized a second school in the town of Nieswiez, province of Minsk, in 1900. Here he faced the same difficulty as in Mir; the local intelligentsia favored either Hebrew or Russian. Among the intellectuals were the Halpern brothers, Falk and Boris. Falk Halpern later became a well-known Hebrew and Yiddish writer, a pedagogue and author of both Hebrew and Yiddish textbooks. Also in Nieswiez was Leon Slonimsky, later a Zionist official in Vilna and a Hebrew pedagogue in New York. Mishkowsky writes:

> I was of the opinion that practically and pedagogically instruction should be in our language. I was also for Yiddish because I was convinced that by using our mother tongue, we would obtain better results in a shorter time than by using either Hebrew or Russian. I maintained that if Russian should be used as the language of instruction in the Jewish school, then why not send the children to the general Russian school? Why separate Jewish schools? After many debates it was decided that the new school be trilingual; Hebrew,

Yiddish, and Russian would be taught. But actually it was a Yiddish school, as Hebrew and Russian were taught as languages, while all subjects were taught in Yiddish. Russian and Hebrew were also taught in Yiddish because first, the children did not understand any language but Yiddish, and without Yiddish you could not approach them; and secondly the methods of *Ivrit b'Ivrit,* or Russian in Russian, were not known yet.

Mishkowsky further tells:

> The school was secular, progressive; it was not supplementary to some other school, but it was a full school where instruction was given from 9 in the morning till 3 in the afternoon. The curriculum included all the subjects that were taught at that time in the European elementary schools.[2]

Although there were as yet no Yiddish textbooks available, the teachers made use of the collections of poetry by Abraham Reisen and Mark Warshavsky.

To popularize the school, the teachers arranged a concert with singing, dancing, and recitations by the pupils. Poems by Simon Frug, Abraham Reisen, Warshavsky, and by the Russian fable writer, Krylov, were recited; and stories by Mendele Mokher Seforim and Sholem Aleichem were read. The event proved to be a great success. In his recollections, Mishkowsky says: "Then I realized what an important part Yiddish played in our lives. How much happiness, not to mention usefulness, education in Yiddish can give us; and I became yet prouder of my language."[3]

The school had been organized without formal legal approval, but for a while the police tolerated its existence. However, after a rebellion against the officers in the local military garrison, several teachers fled to avoid arrest, and the police then closed the school.[4]

Attempts to open secular schools were made in other towns in the province; Baronowiche, Stolpcy, Gorodye and Zamirie. However, the schools did not last long because of the opposition of the government and police.[5]

Abraham Reisen, in his recollections, tells of a Yiddish school that existed in Warsaw as early as 1899. The school had about thirty pupils, whose curriculum consisted of reading and writing Yiddish, and elementary arithmetic.[6]

Although few Yiddish secular schools were opened before the Revolution of 1905, more and more Jewish teachers realized that

Yiddish was the best medium for secular Jewish education. A conference of teachers of Russian-language Jewish schools was held in Vilna during Passover 1907. The conference had neither government sanction nor police permit, and all the sixty-five participants were arrested and jailed together. But, undaunted, they continued the conference in the Vilna prison. The conference adopted a resolution which stated:

> The idea of a new Jewish school is not only gaining sympathy, but is gradually becoming a fact. In some towns Yiddish was introduced as a language of instruction in the evening schools for adults, and even in a few day schools for children.
> There is a demand now for textbooks and a terminology.[7]

The trend towards Yiddish at that time was so prevalent that even among the students of the extremely Hebraist "Grodno courses" (semi-legal Hebrew Teachers Institute) there were Yiddishists who later occupied important positions in the Yiddish schools.[8]

On their own initiative, individual teachers introduced some instruction in Yiddish and Yiddish literature at various private Russian-language Jewish schools. Such courses in Yiddish were begun in 1912 in girls' schools in Golta, in the province of Kherson. The first teacher of Yiddish there was the present editor of *Davar,* the Hebraist David Zakay.[9]

In the same school, the well-known pedagogues Chaim Kazhdan and Abraham Golomb taught Yiddish, Yiddish literature and language.[10] But the girls' school in Golta was no exception. Gradually teachers began to introduce Yiddish-language and Yiddish-literature courses in the various Russian-Jewish elementary and pre-gimnazia girls' schools. By 1910, Yiddish courses were taught in about thirty-five such schools.[11]

Yiddish language courses were also started in a few community Talmud Torahs where the Jewish subjects and some secular subjects were taught in Russian. A number of these schools introduced the study of Yiddish and used it in teaching some secular subjects, as well.[12]

At about the same time, 1910–1912, the Jewish community *(Kehilah)* of Warsaw opened a number of schools where the secular subjects were taught in Polish. Without the approval of the directors, several teachers began very successfully to teach in Yiddish.[13]

In 1912, a Yiddishist director of a community school in Warsaw converted his school into a secular Yiddish school. The curriculum of this school was based on the Russian type of elementary school. Jewish history and literature were added to the curriculum, and all subjects, including biology, geography, and arithmetic, were taught in Yiddish. Among the teachers in the school were the well-known writers and educators Jacob Levine, Moishe Guttman, Tchemerinsky-Mordkhele, D. B. Slutzky, and M. Birnbaum.[41]

The most important Yiddish secular school, founded in 1911, in a suburb of Kiev, in Demievke, was the Demievke School. Its founders were Bundists and the autonomists, the "Sejmists." The school was legalized as a heder employing a number of teachers *(melamdim)*, which meant that the government paid little attention to it, and had no control over the curriculum. The Demievke School, consisting of five grades, followed the curriculum of the official elementary school. In time, the Demievke became a model school and was visited by many educators, teachers and principals. Through the local branch of the "Mefitse Haskalah" (the dissemination of enlightenment) at first refused to subsidize the school, public pressure compelled it to grant the Demievke a subsidy.[15] The school, which included nearly 150 pupils, existed until it was incorporated into the Soviet Yiddish-school system.

A new development in the field of Jewish education was the evening school for adults. This appeared in the last few years of the nineteenth century and grew rapidly in the first decade of the twentieth century.

Though some licenses to open evening schools for adults were granted prior to 1905, new ones were extremely difficult to get. The school charters called for Russian as the language of instruction. The curriculum was to embrace only the elementary-school program, which included Russian, arithmetic, biology, Jewish history, and Yiddish. The directors and teachers were in constant fear lest the inspectors discover that Yiddish, not Russian, was actually employed, or that the pupils knew more than the program called for.

Evening schools of this type existed in a number of cities, the largest in Warsaw and Vilna. It was estimated by Fialkov that, during the first World War, schools functioned in seventy localities and had an enrollment of over six thousand. The students were between fifteen and twenty years of age, and most, recruited from the working population, had little or no education.

The schools also arranged lectures, often by Yiddish writers. A frequent lecturer at the Warsaw evening school was Y. L. Peretz. The schools had dramatic groups, and every Purim a play was presented.

An all-Russian literary league was founded in 1905, with headquarters at St. Petersburg. The local branches arranged lectures, discussions, literary evenings, and symposiums. Very popular were the *"Kestl Ovntn"* (box evenings). The audience wrote down questions and deposited them in a box; then the invited guest lecturers answered the questions.

Some of the evening schools grew into "Peoples' Universities" —a name given to evening courses for adults. In 1911, the Vilna school ran a series of lectures about Jewish law, according to the Bible and Talmud; the poetry of Simon Frug; mysticism in Hebrew literature; economic condition of the Jews according to Sombart; and regulation of Jewish emigration. Many graduates of these evening schools became teachers in the Yiddish secular schools.[16]

In the last quarter of the nineteenth century and first decade of the twentieth, it became increasingly obvious that the old heder was unable to satisfy the demands of the new epoch. The heder, which taught benedictions, prayers and the Pentateuch, prepared religious Jews for a closed Jewish society. But Russian industrialization, and the rapid growth of industry and commerce even in the Pale of Settlement, required much more of the Jews. A knowledge of elementary arithmetic, certainly the multiplication table, was necessary. Not only Yiddish, but also Russian, both written and spoken, was essential in order to communicate with the majority of the Russian population.

The new group of modernist Jews, anxious to give their children some secular education, could not be satisfied by the religious curriculum of the heder, nor by the heder Metukan, which disregarded secular subjects. The government schools imposed a quota on Jewish children; only a certain percentage of Jewish pupils were accepted in the pre-gimnazias and gimnazias. There were private Jewish schools as well, which consisted of elementary schools: pre-gimnazias and gimnazias.[17] The end of the first decade of the twentieth century found about 30,000 children studying in various Russian-language Jewish schools. This constituted 7½ percent of the Jewish children of school age.[18] The number of Jewish children in government schools—pre-gimnazias and gimnazias, "Real" schools (technical gimnazias)—where percentage quotas were enforced was estimated in 1910 at 49,000 Jewish pupils. These pupils came, for the most part, from wealthy families, for only the wealthy could afford the very high tuition required of the Jews.[19] The percentage of Jewish pupils in these government gimnazias was higher than the percentage of all Jews of the population. Jewish girls made up 14.1 percent of the total enrollment in the gimnazias and 7.6 percent in the pre-gimnazias.[20]

But the thirst for knowledge and the necessity to acquire an education were not thwarted by the limitations of admission. In 1913, the Russian government, alarmed at the growth of the Jewish student population in the government schools, prohibited the establishment of parallel classes in the private Jewish gimnazias, and refused new applications for opening private Russian-language Jewish gimnazias.[21] An important writer of that period, H. D. Horowitz, commented: "Every month, even the narrow path that remained for us to enter the general institutions of learning, is being barred."[22]

An unestimated number of Jewish young men and women studied and prepared for universities as "external students." An external student received his gimnazia education from a private tutor and then took a comprehensive examination covering the full gimnazia course of study. Upon passing this examination, the student received a diploma which made it possible for him to enter a university providing he came within the provisions of the *numerus clausus*. An inquiry taken in 1914 showed that 26.6 percent of the Jewish university students in Russia were previously external students.[23]

In the twentieth century, when the problem of secular Jewish education in Russia became acute, the idea of a Yiddish secular school emerged. The advocates of the Yiddish school developed three major ideological arguments for this type of educational institution.

In a secular school, they argued, the language of instruction should be the native tongue. Thus, it is only logical that the Jewish schools should be taught in Yiddish. It is easier and more direct to approach the child in its own language; one can begin immediately teaching the required and planned courses without first spending time to teach a foreign language. The Russian language would be taught separately as a special subject, because knowledge of it was essential.

The second ideological reason for the secular Yiddish school was to foster socialism. In the secular schools the Bundists, the Zionist-Socialists, saw a means of implanting in the children a socialist approach to life. This view found its full and complete expression in Maria Frumkin's book, which we have analyzed. The cause of nationalism constituted the third ideological reason. The ideologists of the Yiddish secular school maintained that the Jews composed a nationality and, as such, were entitled to the same national rights as all other nationalities. They felt that a folk school in the language of the people was the natural school. The ideologists, waking with the demand and spirit of the changing times, prepared the way for the new secular Jewish school.

Despite opposition by the government and the police, some schools managed to exist. The new law of 1914 permitting the use of the native language for instruction, which was passed by the Duma and approved by the government, finally made possible the legalization of the secular Yiddish schools. However, the local administrations, which controlled the schools, made it extremely difficult to utilize this law. For the most part they simply ignored it. Even the Demievke School still existed officially as a Heder. It was only during the war years, 1914–1917, that the local administrations relaxed and granted permits to establish Yiddish schools, which then grew rapidly in number.[24]

NOTES

1. Noah Mishkowsky, *Main Lebn un Maine Raizes* (My Life and Travels), Vol. I, Chap. 15, pp. 102–108, Mexico City, 1947.

2. *Ibid.*, Chap. 19, p. 126.

3. *Ibid.*, p. 128.

4. *Ibid.*, p. 131.

5. Noah Mishkowsky, "Di Ershte Yidishe Veltlekhe Shuln in Russland" (The First Yiddish Secular Schools in Russia), *Shul-Almanakh*, Philadelphia, 1935, p. 340.

6. Abraham Reisen, "Di Ershte Yidishe Veltlekhe Shul" (The First Yiddish Secular School), *Unzer Shul* (Our School), New York, October 1932.

7. Kazhdan, *op. cit.*, pp. 330–331. S. Niger, *In Kamf far a Nayer Dertsiung* (In the Struggle for a new Education), New York, 1940, p. 19.

8. Among the Yiddishists there were Abraham Golomb, Yokhinson, and Henach Kozakevitch. A. Golomb, *A Halber Yorhundert Yidishe Dertsiung* (A Half Century of Jewish Education), Rio de Janeiro, 1957, p. 35. The "Grodno courses" were transferred first to Slonim, then to Kharkov. In 1917 they were Yiddishized by the Mefitse Haskalah. A. Karun, "The Hebrew Pedagogical Courses in Grodno," *Rishonim*, Tel Aviv, 5696, p. 107.

9. Golomb, *op. cit.*, p. 69.

10. *Ibid.*, pp. 71–73.

11. Kazhdan, *op. cit.*, p. 204.

12. Golomb, *op. cit.*, pp. 57–66.

13. S. Hurwitz-Zalkes, *Amol Iz Geven* (Once Upon a Time), New York, 1950, pp. 22 ff.

14. S. Gilinsky, "Tsu der Geschichte fun Yidishn Shulvezn in Varshe" (On the History of the Yiddish School System in Warsaw), *Shul un Lebn* (School and Life), Warsaw, January 1922.

15. Kazhdan, *op. cit.*, pp. 187 ff. Kazhdan states that Hebrew was not taught in the Demievke, p. 189. In the summer of 1961 the present writer met, in Israel, the veteran pedagogue I. Nachmony, who taught in Russia and later in Palestine and Israel. Mr. Nachmony told me that he taught Hebrew at Demievke. The reason that Hebrew was introduced was because the Mefitse Haskalah granted a subsidy only on condition that Hebrew be taught. Mr. Nachmony gave me a photograph of the pupils and the teachers, taken in 1913. The walls of the school room were decorated with photographs of the Yiddish writers, Mendele Mokher Seforim, Peretz, and Sholem Aleichem. The photograph is now in the archives of the YIVO Institute for Jewish Research. It was reproduced in *Yivo News*, No. 83, New York, July 1962, p. 7.

16. Chaim Fialkov, *Folks Ertsiung* (National Education), Petrograd, 1918. About the evening schools, see pp. 23–34.

17. A pre-gimnazia had a five-year curriculum and its graduates could enter the fifth year of gimnazia. A gimnazia consisted of a nine-year curriculum, the preparatory class plus eight yearly grades. The gimnazia corresponded to an American junior and senior high school and about one year of junior college.

18. "Cultural Activities of Soviet Jews," in *Yidn in F.S.S.R.* (Jews in the Soviet Union), edited by S. Dimanshtein, Moscow, 1935, p. 258.

19. Zevi Scharfstein, *Toledot Ha-Hinukh Be-Isroel*, Vol. I, New York, 1945, p. 395.

20. *Ibid.*

21. H. D. Horowitz, "Review of the Month," in *Di Yidishe Velt*, Vilna, No. 7, July 1913, pp. 139–140.

22. *Ibid.*, p. 140.

23. Jacob Lestschinsky, "Di Yidishe Shtutirndike Yugnt" (The Jewish Student Youth), *Di Yidishe Velt*, Vilna, No. 5, May 1914, p. 262.

24. S. Niger, *In Kamf far a Nayer Dertsiung* (Struggle for a New Education), New York, 1940, pp. 21–22.

CHAPTER 3

Yiddish Schools During
the First World War

W HEN the First World War broke out in August 1914, the
hostilities between Germany and Russia immediately affected the
Jewish population along the front. Warsaw was soon filled with
Jewish refugees from towns near the front. The commander-in-
chief of the Russian army issued an order that all Jews living within
fifty versts (about 33 miles) of the front should leave their homes
immediately. This included the governments of Lublin, Kalisz,
Siedlce, Grodno, Kovno and Suwalki. Since the Pale of Settlement
was already overcrowded, the Russian government permitted the
Jewish refugees to settle outside. Though not officially, by 1914
the Pale of Settlement was practically abolished. Sixty-five thousand Jewish refugees settled in central Russia, in the provinces of
Moscow, Vladimir, Voronezh, Nizhni-Novgorod, Tambov, Orlov,
Kursk, Kaluga, Tula, and Riazan; in the southern states, 35,000
Jewish refugees settled.[1]

After the Jewish refugees had adjusted themselves to life in a
strange community, they began to think about education for their
children. Those who settled in the Jewish communities in the Pale
of Settlement could send their children to the existing hadorim.
But there were no hadorim in the cities of central Russia, nor in

the southern states. The few Jews who lived there previously belonged to the privileged classes, as descendants of the "Nikolai I soldiers" or merchants of the first guild,[2] and sent their children to the Russian government schools.

The Jewish war-relief organization, "Ekopo," and the Petrograd and Moscow committees of the all-Russian Mefitse Haskalah, assisted the refugees in organizing schools for their children. Secular schools with Yiddish as the language of instruction were soon established not only in Warsaw and Vilna, but in Moscow, Petrograd, and in other cities. In 1916, there were forty-two Yiddish secular schools with 6,000 children and 130 teachers in the ten central Russian provinces.[3] Yiddish secular schools and kindergartens were also founded in Vilna and in Warsaw, where the leading spirit in the movement was Y. L. Peretz.[4]

Even then it was not a simple matter to organize the Yiddish secular schools. Religious leaders, such as Rabbi Ozer Grodzenski, insisted on a religious education and fought vigorously for the establishment of Hadorim and Yeshivas in the new Jewish settlements.[5] The Zionists were interested in secular Hebrew schools. Great debates were held at the Mefitse Haskalah concerning the problems of Yiddish and Hebrew.

It should be pointed out that secular Yiddish schools were established in some cities, Vilna, Slutsk, Minsk, for local children as well as refugee children. The Russian army had suffered great defeats, and not only were government institutions and officials evacuated, but also schools and teachers. Thus, while the pupils remained in such cities as Vilna, the gimnazias and pre-gimnazias were evacuated leaving the children without schools. In Vilna a number of secular Yiddish schools were opened which took in local children. These schools existed through the German occupation, from 1915 through 1918, and survived until 1941. Altogether, four Yiddish schools, including a gimnazia, were opened in Vilna.

The curriculum of the schools in Vilna was adopted by the new Yiddish schools in central and southern Russia. It consisted of Yiddish, eight hours per week; arithmetic, four hours per week; gymnasium, drawing, singing games, twelve hours per week; Hebrew was taught two hours a week in the first grade and increased to four hours in the second grade and six hours in the third grade. Russian was taught beginning with the third grade (after Germany occupied Vilna, German was introduced, but this did not apply to the schools in central Russia). Geography and biology were introduced in the third grade.

The schools went through a period of adjustment, during which time the children from the hadorim and Hadorim Metukanim who knew Hebrew and the Bible but not the elementary multiplication table, were introduced to secular schooling. Children from the various Russian and Russian-language Jewish schools, who had received an introduction to mathematics, the Russian language and literature, and had already studied "nature science" (biology), and geography, knew no Hebrew nor any Jewish subjects. The difficulties during the period of adjustment were overcome by the teachers, with their enthusiasm for the new Jewish secular school.[6]

The textbooks that were used were *Di Naye Shul* (The New School) by David Hochberg; *Der Shul Khaver* (The School Friend) by L. Yaffe; *Unzer Naye Shul* (Our New School) by Jacob Levine; and *Dos Yidishe Vort* (The Yiddish Word) by M. Olgin. A textbook of elementary arithmetic was prepared by Bravanrik and Levinson. The Hebrew textbooks that were used were *Tal Boker* (Morning Dew) by Lerner and Berkman, and *Ivrit by* I. Glass and Falk Halpern. For Jewish history, *Our History from the Beginning Until the Destruction of the Second Temple,*[7] by I. Myerson, was available.

Because Yiddish textbooks were not available for geography, "nature science," and general history, these subjects were taught in the form of lectures. In the higher grades, the teachers dictated main outlines of these subjects, which were then hectographed and the "scripts" used as textbooks.[8] By completion of the third grade the pupils had learned how to read and write Yiddish well, could read an elementary book in Hebrew, and knew the decimal system in arithmetic.[9]

It was not an easy task for the secular Yiddish school to break through. In addition to the opposition, mentioned earlier, of the Orthodox elements led by Rabbi Grodzensky, there was also resistance from the assimilatory elements who worked for the Russification of the Jewish people, and from the Hebraists who were interested in a Jewish secular school taught in Hebrew.

Special conferences were held at the Mefitse Haskalah, the organization which supervised and subsidized the schools.[10] At one such conference, held in February 1916, in Petrograd, both the Hebraists and the Yiddishists present participated vigorously.

The chief spokesman for the Hebraists was Hayyim Naḥman Bialik, who spoke in the name of "national interests" and in opposition to making a "cult of Yiddish." He advocated using the "eternal language of the Jewish people" in the new schools. Israel Tsinberg proposed that "religious motifs" should be included in the curriculum.[11]

Nahum Shtif,[12] speaking for the Yiddishists, stated that the Jewish child was an "aim in itself and not a means for some purpose." The aim of the Jewish school should be to give the child an opportunity to develop the natural treasures that it possessed. The Hebraists, he declared, were ready to sacrifice the child in the name of national interests. The normal educational and pedagogical principles, which all nationalities in Russia were fighting for, would be lost. In the past, continued Shtif, the ḥeder was the normal Jewish school; but now it has become obsolete, and

> the Hebraists who are concerned with national existence, do not want to utilize the human means that can guarantee the existence of each nation, and are concentrating on Hebrew and maintain that twelve hours a week of Hebrew instruction will save the Jewish people from disappearing.[13]

The educational supervisor of the Mefitse Haskalah said:

> Had the Mefitse Haskalah listened and paid attention to the anti-Yiddish arguments, and opened schools for the refugee children according to the Hebrew or Russification programs, such action would have been a betrayal not only of the interests of the Jewish people but also of the national interests of all nationalities of Russia who strive and struggle for a real national school.[14]

The inspector of the schools in the Tambov and Nizhni-Novgorod region, Falk Halpern, reported: "In the cities where the Orthodox elements opened ḥadorim according to the old curriculum of prayers, Chumash with Rashi, these schools remained empty. The small school with the 'storybooks'[15] cannot take in all children who apply."[16]

The conference at Petrograd adopted the following resolutions:

A. In the schools for refugee children all subjects should be taught in Yiddish except Russian, the history of Russia, and the geography of Russia which, according to the law of July 1, 1914, must be taught in Russian.

B. Hebrew is to be taught either in Hebrew or Yiddish.

C. Jewish history should be taught in Yiddish—but on special occasions it may be taught in Hebrew.

D. Yiddish is not only to be used for instruction, but should be taught as a separate subject.

E. The religious element must occupy a position in the school.

F. Hebrew should be taught to the extent that, upon graduation, the pupils should be able to understand a Hebrew book.

After the resolutions had been adopted, Nahum Shtif proposed a motion that all Jewish folk schools, including those for non-refugee children, should incorporate them. But the conference decided that it was qualified to deal only with the schools for refugee children.[17]

The Moscow branch of the Mefitse Haskalah which had met previously, on November 1, 1915, had issued this statement:

> The Jewish school saved Judaism and the Jewish people two thousand years ago—and now our schools can do the same, save our Polish-Lithuanian Jewish culture. Our schools should continue the tradition of the heder, and use Yiddish as the language of instruction, utilizing the School Law of July 1, 1914. But in our schools we must teach the Bible, Jewish history and—together with these—Russian and secular subjects.[18]

N. Sokolowski,[19] who was then a territorialist,[20] spoke in behalf of the new schools at the conference on November 25:

> We aim to create a secular school. Yiddishists strive to create, in Yiddish, a national culture. In our past we have given the world the Bible. In the future we will give the world another such book. The Jewish secular school in the native language is the real medium to create great opportunities for our national culture.[21]

Although the Jewish secular schools were legal, even subsidized by the Imperial Fund, no pedagogical conferences were permitted. However, early in 1916 a secret teachers' conference was held in Tambov, where some problems of the schools were discussed. The chief speakers at the conference were Falk Halpern, David Hochberg, and Henach Kozakevitch.[22]

Among the resolutions that this conference adopted were the following:

> Taking into consideration that the Jewish [Yiddish] School must have in mind, besides the intellectual development, the energy and activity of the child; we stress that the new Jewish School, all sub-

jects taught in the School, and the methods used to transmit the education, must strive to awaken initiative in the children in all fields.

With regard to the language, the resolution adopted read:

> The Yiddish language is the dominating language in the Folk
> School, its prevalence must not be limited. The Yiddish language
> and its literature should be taught according to the proportion of the
> other subjects. For the upper grades, where literature is taught, two
> hours a week should be spent in teaching reading and writing, and
> two hours a week should be spent for literary readings. It is sug-
> gested that special time, outside the classroom hours, be devoted to
> literature readings. The conference also recommended that slides
> about literary topics be prepared.[23]

As for the teaching of Hebrew, the conference adopted a resolution
which read:

> We recognize that Hebrew should be taught in the Yiddish
> School, and it should occupy a proper place in the curriculum: in
> the first grade it should be taught four hours a week, in the second,
> third and fourth grades six hours a week, and in the fifth and sixth
> grades eight hours a week.[24]

The Jewish writers and officials of the various Jewish organizations of that period paid a great deal of attention to the problems
of the schools and education. A Yiddish writer and leader of the
Socialist-Zionist party, Dobin-Shimoni, wrote an essay that reads
in part:

> The Jewish School aims to develop the Jewish child and make
> him a participator in the events of the day. The School aims to
> make a Jew of the child, a member of the Jewish community and,
> therefore, Jewish subjects should be taught. Our life is dual. We
> are surrounded both by the national community and by non-Jewish
> surroundings. Our soul is dual, it is both Jewish and universal—
> and our schools must also be dual. Both Jewish and non-Jewish
> subjects must be taught. The Hebraists aim to build a nationalist
> Jewish School. The National, the free, the integrated school will be
> built by the Yiddishists.[25]

Another writer, S. Niger, in an article entitled "The Island,"
stressed the importance of national culture.

> Each new Jewish school, each new Jewish library, each cultural
> association outside the pale of settlement constitutes not an ordinary

cultural act, but is an act of national survival, a ring in the chain of our national cultural work. Each new cultural institution strengthens the new settlements and also helps to build a bridge from the old, from the National Island to the National Continent.[26]

An author, who signed his article with the pen name R. Zeura, summarized the accomplishments and the problems of the new Jewish School.

> On July 1, 1914, a law was promulgated allowing all nationalities to open schools in their native tongues. For the first time an opportunity presented itself to found Yiddish Folk Schools. Now our problem of education can be solved—and now the problem to provide our people with proper elementary schools can be taken up. ... We can establish now our public school system, but we lack all necessary preparations: we are short of teachers, of textbooks; we have no experience and no program. In normal times the Law of July 1, 1914, would have pointed out more sharply our Jewish tragedy.

> But now, Jews have been taken out from their own environment and have been settled in Central Russia. And in these provinces we have not one or two—but many schools where the language of instruction is the Jewish native tongue. Over 5,000 children have the opportunity to get acquainted with the surrounding environment, with the life and history of the Jewish people in the language that they have been familiar with since their cradles. Who can appreciate how much joy and how many good hopes this fact brings into our life?

> Two main objectives have been won: The Yiddish Folk School became a recognized fact in the all Russian school system and the Mefitse Haskalah, that is called upon to concentrate its activities for Jewish folk education, has recognized that Yiddish is the language of instruction in the Jewish folk school. This way a long standing struggle has been solved. Now we must concentrate on the training of teachers and producing the proper textbooks.[27]

NOTES

1. "Fun Tog tsu Tog," Petrograd, February 1916, *Vestnik* (Bulletin) of the Moscow branch of the Jewish Relief Committee for War Victims, No. 4, September 27, 1916 (Russian).

2. A bona-fide merchant, who purchased an annual business patent for a sum of 2,000 rubles.

3. *Vestnik,* same issue.

4. About the schools in Warsaw, consult: Miriam Eisenstein, *Jewish Schools in Poland, 1919–1939,* New York, 1950, pp. 18 ff. For Vilna: Moishe Schalit,

Vilner Kulturele Anshtaltn (Vilna Cultural Institutions), Vilna, 1916; Chaim Pupko, "Vilna—the Cradle of the Yiddish Secular School," in the collection *Vilna,* edited by Y. Yeshurin, New York, 1935, pp. 296–299.

5. *Evreiskie Vesti* (Jewish News), Moscow, No. 7, February 16, 1917.

6. Moishe Schalit, *op. cit.,* pp. 27 ff.

7. Original title: *Unzer Geshikhte, fun dem onheib bizn Khurbn fun Bais Sheni.*

8. M. Schalit, *op. cit.,* p. 32.

9. *Ibid.,* p. 37.

10. The budget of the schools was supplied by Mefitse Haskalah, the Ekopo Relief Committee, and the Tatiana Fund for Refugees, which was the Russian fund sponsored by the Tsar's daughter, Tatiana.

11. Israel Zinberg (1876–1938), author of *History of Jewish Literature.*

12. N. Shtif, Yiddish literary historian and philologist.

13. J. Becker, "Konferents fun Mefitse Haskoleh" (Conference of Mefitse Haskalah), in *Tsum Moment,* Petrograd, February 1916.

14. *Ibid.*

15. A derisive name for the Yiddish school because these schools concentrated on teaching literature (stories, not religion).

16. J. Becker: in *Tsum Moment,* see note 13.

17. *Ibid.*

18. *Evreyskaia Zhizn* (Jewish Life), Moscow, No. 18, November 1, 1915.

19. 1917–1919, leader of the United Jewish Socialist Labor Party (S.S.), Zionist-Socialists. Later joined the Communist Party and worked as a specialist in the Soviet cooperatives. He disappeared during the great purges of 1936–1938.

20. A member of the Jewish Territorialist Organization whose aim was the establishment of an autonomous Jewish homeland in some unoccupied territory other than Palestine.

21. *Evreyskaia Zhizn,* Moscow, No. 20, November 29, 1915, columns 21–25.

22. David Hochberg (1880–?) disappeared in Russia. Henach Kozakevitch, a graduate of the Grodno Courses, was a teacher, writer and editor. He joined the Communist Party and became editor of the Kiev daily, *Di Komunistishe Fon (The Communist Flag).* He died in Birobidzhan.

23. *Vestnik Evreyskovo Prosveshchenia* (Courier of Jewish Education), No. 42, March 1916, Petrograd.

24. *Ibid.*

25. *Dos Naye Lebn* (The New Life), Petrograd, 1916 (no other date given).

26. "Di Vispe" (The Island), in *Dos Naye Lebn,* Petrograd, 1916.

27. R. Zeura in *Dos Yidishe Vort,* January 1916, Petrograd. The number of children that the writer mentions is that of the schools in central Russia, and does not include the children in the Yiddish schools in German-occupied territories, Warsaw, Vilna, etc.

CHAPTER 4

Yiddish Schools During the Revolutionary Years 1917–1918

THE Russian Revolution of March 1917 abolished Tsarism—and with it all Jewish restrictions. In the first Manifesto of March 15, 1917, the Provisional Government proclaimed the abolition of all restrictions imposed upon national and religious groups. On April 2, 1917, a law was promulgated which stated: "All restrictions imposed upon the rights of Russian citizens by legislative acts now in force and based upon their adherence to a particular religious faith, religious sect, or nationality are herewith repealed."[1]

The abolition of anti-Jewish regulations and restrictions was greeted by all Jews with great joy and, in their newly won freedom, their pent-up energies were released and great creativity was displayed. Jewish political parties became active. New Yiddish dailies appeared in Petrograd, Kiev, and Minsk. Publishing houses sprang up in Petrograd, Moscow, Kiev, Odessa, and Minsk. While the various Jewish political parties—the Socialist Labor Bund, the Poale Zion, the United Jewish Socialist Labor Party, the General Zionists, the Zeire Zion, Mizrahi, Agudat Israel, the People's Party (Folk's Party) and the People's Group—conducted a struggle among themselves for hegemony of Jewish social, political, and cultural life, all parties agreed that the Jews should have national cultural autonomy, recognized by the government, which should establish a Jewish educational system.

The Provisional Government, harassed by the war and by the Bolsheviks, had no opportunity to pass a law about national cultural autonomy for the nationalities. But in September 1917, it issued a statement of policy which set forth its aims as:

> Recognition of the right of self-determination for all nationalists, under such conditions as shall be determined by the Constituent Assembly. Drafting and promulgation of laws that shall guarantee to national minorities, in the places of their permanent residence, the free use of their native tongues in schools, courts, and organs of self-government, and in their relations with the local organ of the central government.

> Establishment of a council for national affairs attached to the Provisional Government, in which all the nationalities of Russia shall be represented and which shall prepare materials on the national question for the Constituent Assembly.[2]

The Jewish political parties made preparations to call an all-Russian Jewish congress for the purpose of establishing an organization to coordinate all Jewish educational and communal activities, and represent the national Jewish cultural autonomy.

All Russian political parties, except the Bolsheviks, supported the idea of national cultural autonomy for the minority peoples. During the first, and only, session of the Constituent Assembly that was held in January 1918, the chairman of the Assembly, Victor M. Chernov, declared:

> The Jewish people, which has no continuous territory of its own, shall be entitled equally with the other peoples to fashion, on the territory of the Russian Republic, organs of national self-government and to express in these the will of its active elements.[3]

The people of the Ukraine, where the majority of the Jews lived, moved to establish an autonomous Ukrainian Republic.[4] The national cultural autonomy of the Jewish minority was recognized as soon as the Ukrainian autonomous republic was constituted.[5]

During the eight months, March 13–November 7, of the existence of the Russian Provisional Government, the Jewish educational system went through a great transformation. The ḥadorim were closing down. Because the "percentage quota" had been abolished, Jewish pupils entered the gimnazias in great numbers. Pupils entered the Yiddish secular schools, where only refugee children had previously been enrolled, and new schools, both Yiddish and Hebrew, were opened in all Jewish towns. Some of the Russian-language Jewish elementary schools, pre-gimnazias and gimnazias adopted either Hebrew or Yiddish as the language of instruction.

By the time the new school year began to develop, the Bolsheviks seized power, and all the schools, both Russian and minority language, were incorporated into the new Soviet school system. However, early in 1918, the German army occupied both Belorussia and the Ukraine. The schools which were established there during the days of the Provisional Government in 1917 managed to survive under the various occupations which followed the evacuation of the German army in November 1918. It was only at the end of 1920, after both the civil war and the Russo-Polish war were over, that the Soviet government finally took over all the Jewish schools and began to transform them into Soviet schools.

At the all-Russian Zionist Conference which was held in May 1917, in Petrograd, the following resolution was adopted:

> The language of instruction in all schools and educational institutions of the communities should be Hebrew. This rule does not apply to the instruction of the government language and other languages. The Hebrew language is the official language of all public institutions of the Hebrew nation (Ha-am ha-yivri).
>
> The Congress urges all Zionist groups to work for the enforcement of these rules in the community organizations and all the institutions. In the event, if for local and temporary reasons, the introduction of Hebrew is not possible, and the choice is between a foreign language and Yiddish, Yiddish is preferred.[6]

During that period the Zionists and Hebraists succeeded in establishing the central Tarbut organization, as well as over two hundred schools, teachers' seminaries and various other educational institutions.[7]

Meanwhile, new Yiddish schools were being established throughout Russia. Some of the community Talmud Torahs were converted into secular Yiddish schools.[8]

In July 1917, Maria Frumkin delivered a public address in Minsk, in which she formulated a program for the new secular schools.[9] In an article that she published, she said:

> Now that the working class has reached the road to full develop-
> ment, its cultural aims will be fulfilled. Now the blooming of Yid-
> dish literature, art, and language, and the creation of the new
> democratic Jewish culture will be truly possible.[10]

Meanwhile, in June 1917 an all-Russian conference of Jewish teachers was held in Petrograd. The conference, called by the Petrograd Bureau of the Mefitse Haskalah, was attended by 135 delegates representing 1,784 Jewish teachers. The teachers present were from the Yiddish schools, the Hebrew schools, and the various Russian-language Jewish schools. They discussed the organization of a Jewish Teachers League, and the nature of the Jewish school in the new democratic Russia, the two most important problems.

In opening the conference, the representative of the Mefitse Haskalah, A. Strashun, declared that the Jewish teacher should express his views about the character of the Jewish school. The primary purpose of the conference was to organize a Jewish Teachers Union which would become part of the All-Russian Teachers Union. Secondly the conference hoped to formulate the program for the Jewish School.

Ben Zion Dinur,[11] in his paper, said that the government should recognize Yiddish as the official language of the Jewish people in Russia. In the struggle between Hebrew and Yiddish, the teachers must find a way to synthesize both tendencies and thereby facilitate the further development of the national Jewish culture.

Falk Halpern asserted that the school must be based primarily on pedagogical foundations; the language should be Yiddish, the school should be secular, free, and financed by the government. Hebrew and Hebrew literature would occupy an important place in the curriculum.

A. Strashun maintained that the basic Jewish school should be an eight-year school, secular, obligatory, financed by the govern-ment, with instruction in Yiddish.

The final resolution adopted called for the school to be:

> . . . free, obligatory, and secular. Religion should not be part of the
> curriculum. The language of instruction should be Yiddish. Hebrew
> and Hebrew literature, which constitute such an important element
> in Jewish culture, must occupy an important position in the system
> of Jewish folk education, beginning with the elementary school.

This resolution did not satisfy the Hebraists, and the conference split into two factions. Those who agreed with the official resolution organized themselves into the Jewish Teachers Association; the Hebraists, who demanded the Hebrew language for instruction, organized a separate association, Ha-Moreh, (the Teacher), at a special conference held in Odessa, July 1917.[12]

During the hectic period of the Provisional Government and the first few years of the Bolshevik seizure of power, the Jewish school system grew and developed, as was pointed out previously. Both the Yiddish and the Hebrew schools developed in the Ukraine, which became an autonomous republic.

As early as July 1, 1917, the Central Ukrainian Rada[12A] established a special department for the national minorities in the Ukraine. Moshe Zilberfarb, a leader of the United Jewish Socialist Labor Party (S.S.) became the executive secretary of the Jewish Section.[13]

The Central Rada in the Ukraine recognized the principle of the national cultural autonomy of the Jews, and this principle was incorporated into a law, published on January 9, 1918:

> In agreement of the Universal of November 7, 1917, the Rada states that each nationality living in the Ukraine has, within the borders of the Ukrainian Republic, the right of national personal autonomy; it has the right to organize its national life through organs of a national assembly. This right for personal cultural autonomy is granted to the Great Russian, the Jewish, and Polish nationalities that live within the borders of the Ukraine.[14]

Jewish autonomy was supported by the local organs, the newly elected *Kehilahs,* which were coordinated through the Ministry of Jewish Affairs. They planned to establish a National Jewish Assembly by democratic elections, which would be the chief organ of National Cultural Autonomy.[15]

The Ukraine went through great turmoil during the years 1917–1920. In 1918 it was occupied by the Germans; the democratic Central Rada was abolished and General Pavlo Skoropadski, aided by the German occupation forces, became the dictator of the Ukraine. After the Armistice of November 1918, the Germans left and Skoropadski escaped with them. The Central Rada was reestablished in the city of Vinnitsa and the Law of National Cultural Autonomy was reinstated.[16] The entire Ukraine was plunged into a bloody war when the Bolsheviks invaded from central Russia and various armies and bands fought one another. This was accompanied by anti-Jewish pogroms when thousands of Jews were slain.[16A]

Despite the turmoil and bloodshed, the Ministry of Jewish Affairs continued to exist although the Minister changed. There were four ministers altogether: M. Zilberfarb, V. Latzki, A. Revutsky, and P. Krasny. The Ministry was abolished, as was National Personal Cultural Autonomy and all its organs, when the Communists took over the Ukraine in 1920. But during the period of transition, Jewish schools were established throughout the Ukraine; the Ministry of Jewish Affairs established secular Yiddish schools, while various associations established Hebrew secular schools.[17]

A. Revutsky, the third Minister for Jewish Affairs, issued the following declaration:

> Until the central organs of the National Jewish Assembly will be established according to the Law of National Personal Autonomy of January 9, 1918, all Jewish educational institutions of all types are being transferred to the Ministry of Jewish Affairs.
>
> For the necessities of Jewish education, funds are being assigned from the government finances. The sum corresponds to one-ninth of the total sum spent by the government for education.
>
> Until the exact sum will be fixed for the year 1919 the Ministry of Jewish Affairs will spend five million rubles each month for Jewish education.[18]

The language of the autonomous Jewish culture was Yiddish. All correspondence was conducted in Yiddish, and laws promulgated by the central government were published in Yiddish. The money issued in the Ukraine included a Yiddish text.[19]

Revutsky stated officially:

> We are convinced that the idea of national cultural autonomy loses ground if it is not built on the foundation of one language. The only language with which Jewish cultural autonomy can be built is Yiddish. Schools using other languages than Yiddish cannot get any government subsidies. The same applies to Jewish schools where Hebrew is not taught. We will legalize schools using Hebrew as the language of instruction and secure accreditation for them if they are maintained by private people, parents, or organizations.[20]

The Ministry of Jewish Affairs prepared election regulations for democratic local Kehilas which would organize the local schools,[21] and cooperated with the "Kultur-Lige." This League for Culture was established in the Ukraine by the Jewish political parties, both Yiddishist and semi-Yiddishist: the Folks-Partei (People's Party), the United Jewish Socialist Labor Party, the Jewish Socialist Labor Bund, the Poale Zion.

For a brief period the Kultur-Lige had under its supervision a publishing house, a dramatic studio, forty-two kindergartens, sixty-three elementary schools, three gimnazias, fifty-four libraries, eleven orphanages, and a teachers' seminary.[22] The Teachers' Seminary in Kiev was directed by Dr. Chaye Berenson and had the following faculty:[23]

Simon Dobin	Department of Yiddish
Dr. M. Sester	Department of Hebrew and Bible
Dr. Dinaburg (Dinur)	History
M. Dobin	Biology
M. Dobin and U. Golomb	Physics
Dr. Olga Rein	Mathematics

It was the Kultur-Lige which the Educational Department of the Ministry of Jewish Affairs used to administer the Jewish secular school. It functioned during the Skoropadski dictatorship, when the Ukrainian Rada and the Ministry of Jewish Affairs were both abolished; also during the period of turmoil and the brief Bolshevik occupations. The Kultur Lige was taken over by the Communists when Soviet rule was finally established in the Ukraine.

The Yiddish schools in the Ukraine were secular schools; some were newly founded, and some were converted from the Russian-language Jewish schools. They followed the program of the Russian schools, in which the elementary schools consisted of five grades, and the gimnazias of a preparatory grade followed by eight grades. Yiddish was the language of instruction, but Hebrew and Hebrew literature were subjects of instruction. (It should be pointed out that no Yiddish or Yiddish literature were taught in the Hebrew secular schools.)

In the field of higher education, the Ministry of Jewish Affairs planned the establishment of a Jewish University. In the meantime the Ministry instituted two chairs for Jewish History and Literature at the Ukrainian University in Kamenetz-Podolsk.[24]

A memorandum submitted to the Council of Ministers in June, 1918, by the Ministry of Jewish Affairs stated the condition of Jewish education in the Ukraine. In January 1918 there were 270,000 Jewish children in the Ukraine between the ages of seven and eleven. Of these 96,000 were in both Jewish and non-Jewish secular schools, and 174,000 Jewish children were outside the secular schools, most of them probably in hadorim. According to the memorandum, studying in the Russian schools hindered the development of the Jewish child.

> This poor situation is due to the fact that there was never, in the Ukraine a central school organization to fit the specific conditions, or the psychology and history of the Jewish people. A central school organization should be formed to provide both elementary and secondary schools suitable for Jewish children.

> The Department of Education of the Ministry of Jewish Affairs aims to remedy this situation, and to solve the problem of Jewish education.

The memorandum further stated that the Ministry aimed to keep the local *Kehilahs,* organize and administer new schools; and reform the existing Russian-language Jewish schools that were established according to the law of 1873, and convert them into secular Yiddish schools. The Ministry assigned 50,000 rubles for the publishing of textbooks, and prepared a law to assign an additional half-million rubles for the same purpose.

During the brief period since December 1917, about one hundred gimnazias were founded in the Ukraine by parents' groups and various associations. These gimnazias charged a tuition fee of 400 rubles per year, and therefore only the well-to-do could afford to send their children. The memorandum recommended that, therefore, the government should organize new gimnazias for the children whose parents could not pay the high tuition fee.[25]

However, on July 19, 1918, before any action could be taken, the Ministry of Jewish Affairs was abolished by the hetman, Pavlo Skoropadski. It was revived in Vinnitsa on December 16, 1918, when the Democratic Rada was reinstated. With the approval of his party, Abraham Revutsky, a Poale Zionist, became the new Minister of Jewish Affairs.[26]

During the various changes of regimes in the Ukraine, the Ministry of Jewish Affairs was occupied mainly in seeking means to stop the anti-Jewish pogroms and to grant aid to the victims. It attempted, through the "Culture League," to build a secular Jewish-school system. To encourage this work, the Jewish People's Party issued the following proclamation:

The cultural work that the Peoples' Ministry for Jewish Affairs has started, the publishing activities, and the preparation for opening a Teachers Institute, must not be interrupted. Work should be continued in the same direction.

All means should be taken to strengthen the Jewish public school that is being built on the national foundation of the folk language, Yiddish, and on the principle of secularism. The Ministry of Jewish Affairs must also pay attention to the abnormal conditions of modern Jewish education, which is separated from the people and its culture, and which is dominated by the elements of assimilation. The Ministry of Jewish Affairs has gradually adjusted the Jewish secondary schools to the national demands of the times and Jewish folk interests. The Ministry of Jewish Affairs must take charge of professional training and out-of-school education of the people, organize evening schools, children's homes and libraries. A special department must be established at the Ministry of Jewish Affairs for Jewish professional training to harmonize with the economic necessities and the professional composition of the Jewish folk masses.

The Ministry for Jewish Affairs should adopt means by which the study of the Ukraine and its culture will be included in the Jewish-school-system curriculum.[27]

The newly reestablished Ukrainian Democratic Republic with the Central Rada did not exist long. The Red Army attacked the Ukraine and, although the people fought, by April 1918 the forces of the Rada were defeated. The Ukrainian government fled as early as February 1919, when the Red Army occupied Kiev, the capital. The Minister of Jewish Affairs, Abraham Revutsky, resigned as a protest against the anti-Jewish pogroms, and Krasny was appointed in his place. With the liquidation of the Ukrainian Rada, the Ministry of Jewish Affairs and the Law of National Cultural Personal Autonomy were abolished.

On March 22, 1919, the following memorandum was submitted to the Soviet Commissariat in Kiev:

To the Comrade Commissars:

Six weeks have passed since the Ministry of Jewish Affairs was taken over by the Soviet government. During this period no work has been done by the Department of Education. Inquiries and memoranda have not been acknowledged, nor answered. Thus, the very idea of Jewish public education is being discredited, and its very foundation is being destroyed. We, the officials, do not know what to do. We therefore ask to be relieved of our duties.

> Director of Department of Education, Chaim Fialkov
> Director of Schools, Chaim Kazhdan
> Director of Out-School Department, Noah Lurie
> Director of Publications, Nachman Maisel
> Director of Pre-School Dept., Boris Isurowitch.[28]

The work of the Ministry of Jewish Affairs, and its educational arm, the Kultur-Lige, ceased; and the existing Jewish schools were taken over by the Soviet government.

In later years, Jewish Soviet writers claimed the origin and continuation of the Jewish secular school system for the Soviet government. Thus an official Soviet publication states:

> After the victory of the October Revolution, the Soviet government began the cultural work among the Jewish masses from the foundation.[29]

This propaganda statement is, of course, false; as are all writings which contend that only after the Soviet seizure of power did the Jews in Russia acquire a secular school system. The ideological base for the secular Jewish school system was laid at the beginning of the twentieth century by Jewish Democratic Socialists, Folkists and Yiddishists. Secular schools were opened in Warsaw and Kiev as early as 1910, and despite Tsarist attempts to hamper its growth, the movement was never arrested.

The law of July 1, 1914, which permitted the use of the native language as the language of instruction in the schools, made it legally possible to open Yiddish secular schools. However, the local officials were not anxious to allow the implementation of the law when it came to Yiddish schools. But during the war, Yiddish schools were opened; at first for children of refugees, and then for nonrefugee children, especially in Vilna and Warsaw.

The secular Jewish-school system expanded during the regime of the Democratic Provisional Government, and under the Central Rada in the Ukraine.

The Soviet government took over the secular Yiddish schools, the secular Hebrew schools of the Tarbut, and the private and government Russian-language Jewish schools, and converted them into Soviet Yiddish schools; these at first showed a great expansion. A decline followed later, as a result of the Soviet policy towards the Jews and the Soviet view of Jewish culture.

NOTES

1. Solomon M. Schwartz, *The Jews in the Soviet Union,* Syracuse University Press, 1951, p. 90.

2. *Ibid.,* p. 91.

3. *Ibid.,* p. 92.

4. Robert S. Sullivant, *Soviet Politics and the Ukraine, 1917–1957,* New York, 1962, Columbia University Press, pp. 18–19.

5. M. Zilberfarb, *Dos Yidishe Ministerium un di Yidishe Autonomie in Ukraine* (The Ministry of Jewish Affairs and Jewish Autonomy in the Ukraine), Kiev, 1918.

6. Arya Raphaeli (Tsentsiper), *Be'Maavak Le'Geulah* (In the Struggle for Redemption), Tel Aviv, 1956, p. 24.

7. A. L. Tsentsiper, *Esser Shenot Redifot* (Ten Years of Persecution), Tel Aviv, 1930, p. 39.

8. *Der Veker,* Minsk, February 29, 1919.

9. *Der Veker,* Minsk, July 18, 1917.

10. *Ibid.,* September 21, 1917.

11. Formerly Minister of Education in Israel, then known as Ben Zion Dinaburg. See source in note 12.

12. Zevi Scharfstein, *Toledot ha-Hinukh Be'Yisroel,* Vol. III, New York, 1949, pp. 41–43. Chaim Kazhdan, *Fun Kheyder un Shkoles Biz Tsisho* (From Heder and Schools to Tsisho), Mexico City, 1956, pp. 333–339.

12A. The *rada* was the Ukrainian central council or parliament.

13. S.S. stands for the Russian Socialist Zionists. Actually this was a Territorialist party.

14. M. Zilberfarb, *Dos Yidishe Ministerium un di Yidishe Autonomie in Ukraine* (The Ministry for Jewish Affairs and Jewish Autonomy in the Ukraine), Kiev, 1918, p. 79.

15. Abraham Revutsky, *In di Shvere Teg af Ukraine* (In the Difficult Days in the Ukraine), Berlin, 1924, pp. 191–192.

16. A. Revutsky, *op. cit.,* p. 8.

16A. N. Gergel, "The Pogroms in the Ukraine in the Years 1918–1921"(Yiddish), *Yivo Shriftn far Ekonomie,* Volume I, 1928, pp. 106 ff; S. Dubnov, *Divrei Yemey Am Olam* (World History of the Jewish People), Hebrew, Vol. XI, Tel Aviv, 1940, pp. 8–14; E. Heifetz, *The Slaughter of the Jews in the Ukraine in 1919,* New York, 1921; A. D. Margolin, *Ukraina i politika Antanty,* Berlin, 1921.

17. M. Zilberfarb, *op. cit.,* pp. 10 ff.

18. A. Revutsky, *op. cit.*, pp. 191–192.
19. M. Zilberfarb, *op cit.*, p. 15.
20. A. Revutsky, *op. cit.*, pp. 97–98.
21. A. Strashun, Editor, *Di Yidishe Autonomie un der Natsionaler Sekretariat in Ukraine, Materialn un Dokumentn* (Jewish Autonomy and the National Secretariat, Materials and Documents), Kiev, 1920, pp. 1 ff.
22. Chaim Kazhdan, *op cit.*, p. 437.
23. A. Golomb, *A Halber Yorhundert Yidishe Dertsiung* (A Half Century of Jewish Education), Rio de Janeiro, 1957, p. 97.
24. A. Revutsky, *op. cit.*, pp. 174, 194.
25. M. Zilberfarb, *op. cit.*, pp. 34–35, 41.
26. A. Revutsky, *op. cit.*, p. 19.
27. M. Zilberfarb, *op. cit.*, Supplement, pp. 83–85.
28. Revutsky, *op. cit.*, p. 181.
29. *Yidn in F.S.S.R.* (Jews in the U.S.S.R.), edited by S. Dimanshtein, Moscow, 1935, p. 257.

CHAPTER 5

Bolshevism and the Jewish School

LENIN'S concern with the Jews and their problems began in 1903, fourteen years before the Bolsheviks seized power, when he clashed with the Jewish Labor Bund whose objectives were: (a) Autonomy for the Bund within the Russian Social Democratic Labor Party. (b) The recognition of the Jews as a nationality, culturally autonomous in the future democratic Russia. Lenin denied that the Jews constitute a nationality, and saw the solution to the Jewish problem in complete assimilation with the majority populations in each country.[1]

Lenin was influenced in his thinking by Karl Kautsky,[2] who stated at that time that the "Jews have ceased to be a nation, for a nation is inconceivable without a territory." After losing their territory, the Jews lived in a unique situation; aliens with strong emotional ties to a homeland which they did not control. Kautsky maintained that anti-Semitism would be eliminated if the Jews merged with the mass of population, and he concluded that this after all "is the only possible solution of the Jewish problem and everything helping to break down Jewish seclusion should be supported."[3]

In 1903 Lenin wrote in one of his articles:

The Bund's argument, which consists of invoking the idea of a Jewish nation, indubitably raises a question of principle. Unfortunately, however, this Zionist idea is entirely false and reactionary in its essence. "The Jews ceased to be a nation, for a nation is inconceivable without a territory," says one of the most outstanding Marxist theoreticians, Karl Kautsky. Also, more recently, in his analysis of the problem of nationalities in Austria, the same writer, attempting to furnish a scientific definition of nationality, lays down two fundamental criteria for this concept, language and territory. The only thing perhaps remaining to the Bundists is to elaborate the idea of a separate Russian Jewish nationality, having Yiddish for its language and the Jewish Pale for its territory.

The idea of a separate Jewish people, which is utterly untenable scientifically, is reactionary in its political implications. The incontrovertible empirical proof is furnished by the well-known facts of history and of the political reality of today. Everywhere in Europe the downfall of medievalism and the development of political freedom went hand in hand with the political emancipation of Jews, their substituting for Yiddish the language of the people among whom they lived, and in general their indubitably progressive assimilation by the surrounding population.

The Jewish question is this exactly, assimilation or separatedness? And the idea of a Jewish nationality is manifestly reactionary, not only when put forward by its consistent partisans (the Zionists), but also when put forward by those who try to make it agree with the ideas of Social Democracy (the Bundists). The idea of a Jewish nationality is in conflict with the interests of the Jewish proletariat for, directly or indirectly, it engenders in its ranks a mood hostile to assimilation, a ghetto mood.[4]

Ten years later, in 1913, Lenin wrote in stronger terms about the Jewish problem:

Out of ten and a half million Jews throughout the world, about one half live in a civilized world, under conditions favoring maximum assimilationism, whereas only the wretched and oppressed Jews of Russia and Galicia, deprived of legal rights and downtrodden by Russian and Polish Purishkeviches [name of a well-known anti-Semite], live under conditions favoring minimum assimilation and maximum segregation, which includes the Pale of Settlement, the numerus clausus and similar Purishkevich delights.

In the civilized world, the Jews are not a nation, there they have achieved the highest degree of assimilation, say Kautsky and Otto

Bauer.[5] In Galicia and Russia the Jews are not a nation! There they are, unfortunately, not through any fault of theirs, but through that of the Purishkeviches, still a caste. Such is the indisputable opinion of men who indisputably know the history of the Jews.[6]

Lenin was adamant in his opinion of Jewish culture and its supporters:

Anyone defending the slogan of national culture belongs among the nationalistic petty bourgeoisie and not among the Marxists. This is also true of the most oppressed and persecuted, the Jews. Jewish national culture is the slogan of the rabbis and bourgeoisie, the slogan of our enemies. Anyone directly or indirectly putting forward the slogan of Jewish national culture is (whatever his good intentions) an enemy of the proletariat, a partisan of the old, and the castelike in the Jewish group, an accomplice of the rabbis and bourgeoisie. Contrariwise, those Jewish Marxists who merge with the Russian, Lithuanian, Ukrainian, and other workers in international Marxist organizations, contributing their share (in both Russian and Yiddish) to the creation of an international culture of the labor movement—those Jews carry on (in defiance of the separatism of the Bund) the best Jewish tradition when they combat the slogan of national culture.[7]

Lenin was confronted with the problem of Jewish schools and education when the superintendent of the Odessa school region proposed a plan, in 1913, to establish separate Jewish schools. Lenin declared the plan reactionary, an attempt "to close the doors of the schools to the Jews." He said that "it is in the interests of the working class to unite the children of all nationalities in integrated schools." Lenin continued:

The damaging project to nationalize the Jewish schools shows how incorrect is the plan of the so-called cultural national autonomy, to take away the school system from the government and to transfer it to each nationality separately. We must not aim for this, but for the unity of the workers of all nationalities in the struggle against all nationalism, in the struggle for a truly democratic public school and for political freedom generally. The example of the progressive countries of the world—let us say Switzerland in Western Europe, and Finland in East Europe—shows us that only integrated, democratic public government institutions insure the human (not animal) integration of various nationalities, without unrealistic and damaging divisions of the school system according to nationalities.[8]

Lenin ridiculed the idea of national cultural autonomy and separate school systems in an article published in December 1913, entitled "The Composition of the Children in the Russian School." He showed that in the region of Petersburg there were Russian, Polish, Czech, Lithuanian, Latvian, French, Italian, German, Swedish, Norwegian, Gypsy, Jewish, Georgian, and Estonian children. He asked how one could organize separate schools for so many nationalities. In the Petersburg school district, twenty-three separate school systems would have to be established to satisfy the demands of national cultural autonomy.

> We must not be concerned about how to place the children in separate school systems, but how to create democratic conditions for all nationalities to live together on a basis of equality.
> It is not national culture that we must proclaim; indeed, we must expose the clerical and bourgeois nature of this slogan in the name of international culture of the international labor movement. . . . To agitate for separate schools for each national culture is reactionary; only under conditions of real democracy can the teaching of one's own history in one's native language be insured, not by dividing the schools according to nationalities. Preaching national cultural autonomy, which cannot be realized, is foolish, and it divides the workers now. Preaching the fusion of the workers of all nationalities makes the achievement of proletarian class solidarity easier, and this can guarantee equality and the peaceful coexistence of all nationalities.[9]

However, in the same article Lenin says that children whose native tongue is other than Russian, who want to study their native tongue and native history, should be able to study after school hours in "a government local and at government expense."

In another article, "Once More About the Division of the School System According to Nationalities," published in December 1913, Lenin reiterates his stand:

> We do not want to fit in socialism with nationalism. We defend full democracy, full freedom and equality of languages; at the same time we do not defend the transfer of the school system to the various nationalities, nor do we defend the division of the school system according to nationalities.[10]

Stalin, in his article "Marxism and the National Question" published in 1913, repeated in a crude form Lenin's views regarding

Jews and Jewish culture, denying that the Jews constituted a nationality:

> The point is, first of all, that the Jews have no large and stable stratum established on the soil, which would hold the nation together in a natural way serving not only as its framework but also as a "national" market. Out of five or six million Russian Jews, only 3 to 4 percent are connected with agriculture in any way. The remaining 96 percent are engaged in commerce, industry, municipal service and generally live in cities; moreover, scattered over Russia as they are, they do not constitute a majority in a single province.
>
> Thus interspersed as national minorities in areas inhabited by other nationalities, the Jews chiefly serve foreign nations as manufacturers and traders and as members of the liberal professions, naturally adapting themselves to the foreign nations in respect to language, etc. All this, together with the increasing mobility of nationalities characteristic of higher forms of capitalism, leads to the assimilation of the Jews. The destruction of the Pale of Settlement will merely serve to hasten assimilation.
>
> The question of national autonomy for the Russian Jews, acquires then a curious character: autonomy is proposed for a nation, whose future is denied, and whose existence has yet to be proven.[11]

Stalin defined nationality as "a historically evolved, stable community of language, territory, economic life and mental constitution expressed in a community of culture."[12] Moreover, Stalin insisted that "it is only when all these characteristics are present that we have a nation."[13] The Jews, by definition, were excluded from his conception of nationality. Stalin, in a subsection of the same article, entitled "The Bund, its Nationalism and its Separatism," ridiculed the very idea of Jewish culture, and the "Spirit of Sabbath."

> The Social Democrats are struggling for the introduction of a compulsory rest day in the week. But the Bund is not satisfied with it. It demands that for the Jewish proletariat Sabbath Rest should be guaranteed in a judicial way. It can be expected that the Bund will take another step forward and will demand the right to celebrate all Jewish holidays. And if the Jewish workers have liberated themselves, to the misfortune of the Bund, from these prejudices, and do not want to celebrate, the Bund, with its agitation for the Right of Sabbath, will remind them [the Jewish workers] of the Sabbath and will cultivate in them the Sabbath Spirit.

It is therefore easy to understand the fiery speeches at the VIII
conference of the Bund, with the demand for Jewish hospitals; and
this demand is justified by their explanation that just as the sick person feels better among his own, the Jewish worker will feel better
among Jewish shopkeepers, than among Polish workers.

To maintain everything that is Jewish, to conserve all national
separateness of the Jews, including that which is clearly harmful for
the proletariat, to separate the Jew from everything which is not
Jewish—to organize even separate Jewish hospitals—this is to what
the Bund has sunk.[14]

The above quotations indicate clearly that both Lenin and Stalin
believed in complete assimilation. Lenin's program consisted of
the abrogation of all legal restrictions imposed upon the Jews by
the Tsarist regime and the establishment of equality before the law.
This remained the basic Bolshevik doctrine regarding the Jews
and neither Lenin nor Stalin modified their views. Even when
Jewish districts were established in the Ukraine and Crimea, and
even when Birobidzhan was established as a Jewish autonomous
province (oblast), the doctrine of assimilation was maintained. It
is true that some Soviet dignitaries and some Jewish communists
later spoke about a "Soviet Jewish Nationality," to justify the
establishment of autonomous Jewish districts and provinces created
for expediency, but the basic Bolshevik conception remained
unchanged. Stalin's opinions concerning the Jews did not waiver,
in spite of Kalinin's statement in later years:

> You ask me why the Jewish autonomous district has been organ-
> ized? I am one of those that has sympathized with the organization
> of this district [Birobidzhan]. The main reason is that there are
> many Jews among us, but they have no state structure. This is the
> only nationality in the U.S.S.R. that has a population of three mil-
> lion and has no state structure. I am of the opinion that the creation
> of such a district, under these conditions, is the only means for a
> normal state development of the nationality. I expect that in ten
> years from now the Birobidzhan autonomous district will be devel-
> oped into a great Socialist construction and, simultaneously, a truly
> Jewish Socialist culture, and those to whom this is dear, those to
> whom such a Socialist Jewish culture is dear, will want to help de-
> velop the Jewish district and its Socialist National Culture—and
> they have to affiliate with Birobidzhan and help it. I think that with
> us the Jews will survive longer as Jews in their own district than
> anywhere else.[15]

Moishe Litvakov, editor of the Moscow daily *Der Emes,* wrote a long article in 1936, in connection with the celebration of the nineteenth anniversary of the Communist Revolution, submitting that under the Soviet regime the Jews were emerging as a nation. He discussed both Lenin's and Stalin's views of the Jewish Question, and showed how correct they were. The Jews were not a nationality under Tsarism, but now:

> The socialist Revolution under the great leadership of the Bolshevik party, with Lenin and Stalin at the head, has accomplished the changing of the social structure of the Jewish population—it has transformed this population into a working people—and in the frame of the working Jewish population, it created a group that it did not possess—a collective-farm population and an industrial proletariat. . . . Gradually the October Revolution has transformed the history of the Jews into a Jewish History, a national history of the Jewish nation . . . and Stalin's formula, national in form, international in content, must be applied in this situation. Because it is a history of the Jewish people that is being transformed, in the U.S.S.R., into a nation.[16]

Another Jewish Communist ideologue, A. Brakhman, wrote in 1936:

> The Bolshevik Party under the great leadership of Lenin and Stalin, fought the reactionary idea of a Jewish nationality. Only the close union of the Jewish workers and toilers with the workers and toilers of all Russia, only the unified struggle against Tsarism, feudalism, the Jewish rabbis, and the wealthy could truly liberate the Jewish masses together with all slaves of Tsarist Russia, from their own and foreign yokes. The road to the Socialist revolution was through the complete liquidation of feudalism and medievalism. The road to social and national liberation of the Jewish masses, the road to the consolidation of a Jewish nationality under the aegis of the proletariat, the road to a Jewish Soviet statehood, to the Jewish autonomous region, the future Jewish Socialist Soviet Republic lay through the liquidation of Jewish medievalism, through the destruction of the Jewish *caste,* through fighting Zionism, Bundism and all other kinds of nationalism. Through all these were created new socialist possibilities, a new historical situation was prepared, the creation of the autonomous Jewish region—the base for a Jewish nation. In this lies the strength and the real greatness of Lenin's—Stalin's dialectic—of the proletarian-revolutionary theory of the practice of Marxism-Leninism.[17]

The expression of such ideas was permitted, but the Bolshevik Party, and Stalin, did not encourage it. All those ideologists who tried to interpret Lenin's and Stalin's views were subsequently executed as nationalists, spies, and the like. The Bolshevik doctrine as expressed by Lenin and Stalin in 1903–1913 remained official. But the problem arose of how to apply this policy to the necessities and demands of the period.

On November 15, 1917, the Council of Peoples' Commissariats presented a Declaration of the Rights of the Peoples of Russia which guaranteed:

1. The equality and sovereignty of the peoples of Russia.
2. The right of the peoples of Russia to free self-determination, even to the point of separation and the formation of an independent state.
3. The abolition of all national religious privileges and limitations.
4. The free development of national minorities and ethnographic groups living on Russian territory.[18]

If certain rights were guaranteed not only to national minorities but also to ethnographic groups, something should be done for the castelike Jews, who numbered in the millions and constituted a major element in the cities of Ukraine and Belorussia. The Bolsheviks wanted to overcome the reluctance of the Jewish people towards the Communists, and to win over at least some of the leaders of the various Jewish political parties and organizations. Without changing their conception of the solution of the Jewish problem, the Communists did make certain concessions. They established a commissariat for Jewish affairs, and Jewish sections of the Communist Party. At the first conference of the Jewish sections of the Communist Party and the local sections of the Jewish Commissariats, held in October 1918, S. Dimanshtein, the Commissar of Jewish Affairs, said:

> The general Russian Communist Party cannot conduct its activities in different languages. Jewish Communist sections have to be set up. The sections have to face a dual task: on the one hand the purely technical assignment of propagandizing among the Jewish masses, on the other hand, to carry through the dictatorship of the proletariat in the Jewish street [among the Jews]. The new Jewish sections will consist of new comrades, who now enter the party. The old Bolsheviks will undoubtedly remain in the general party; we

must therefore see to it that the sections should remain free of petty bourgeois nationalistic trends.

Our main task is to carry through in practice everything that the Communist Party undertakes to do. We are not a special party existing by itself, but a part of the Communist Party that consists of Jewish workers. Being internationalists, we do not set ourselves any special national tasks, but pure class-proletarian tasks. As much as we speak a separate language, we are obligated to see that the Jewish masses have an opportunity to satisfy all their spiritual needs in that language.

We are also not fanatics of the Yiddish language. It is not, for us, a "Yiddish 'ha-kodesh' "[19] as it is for our Jewish nationalists. No, the language for its own sake is not important to us. Our task is to bring together the workers of all nationalities and to unite them in one international family. Our Jewish Communist sections must, in organizational matters, function inside the party organization of each city and in the common committee. The party cards must be obtained from the same committee as all other members of the Communist Party.[20]

Thus the Commissar of Jewish Affairs made it clear that the aim of the Jewish Communists was to extend and enforce the dictatorship of the proletariat among the Jews; propagandize Communism among the Jews; and use Yiddish, because it was the language spoken by the Jews. Yiddish, as a language, however, was to be considered neither holy nor important.

The conference adopted the following resolution about "our cultural tasks":

Education has always been a strong weapon in the hands of the ruling classes. With all the hypocritical arguments of the bourgeoisie that both the school and education should be above class interests and outside of politics, the bourgeoisie has always used its power to prevent the masses from acquiring an education.

Among the Jews [in the Jewish Street], all kinds of petty bourgeois controlled education, and they strove to veil the Jewish masses with Hebrew culture. They [the middle class] sent their children to the general schools, while for the masses they left the dark, crowded Hadorim and Talmud Torahs that brought up ignoramuses.

Only the proletariat, that defends its class interests, defending also the interests of the whole of humanity, can open all treasures of human culture to the masses.

Only the proletariat is capable of forming the golden chain of human culture, tearing it from the hands of the decaying, dying bourgeoisie.

Only the Jewish worker and the toiling masses will create the free Jewish culture, which will give the Jews the best weapons of science.[21]

The same conference adopted another resolution on "our attitude to the Kehilahs and the rest of the bourgeois institutions." The text of the resolution reads:

The first conference of the Jewish Commissariats and of the Jewish sections declares that all institutions which previously functioned in the Jewish Street, the Kehilahs, elected in the well-known fourtail way [universal, equal, direct, and secret], are harmful and have no more room in our life. At a time of perilous struggle, no compromises can be made with the bourgeoisie, and the Jewish masses must not be lulled with sweet songs of so-called democracy.

The Jewish proletariat, leaning on the victory of the proletariat and the October Revolution, forces of power in its hands, proclaims the dictatorship of the proletariat on the Jewish Street, and calls upon all Jewish workers to unite around the Jewish commissariat to strengthen its dictatorship.

The first all-Russian conference of the Jewish commissariat and the Communist sections empowers the collegium of the Central Commissariat for Jewish Affairs to take action for a systematic liquidation of the bourgeois institutions.[22]

The decree abolishing the Jewish community organizations was drafted in April 1919, but its publication was delayed for about two months, because the commissariat had no personnel to administer the various community institutions.[23]

The text of the decree was promulgated:

The central commissariat for Jewish national affairs, having acquainted itself with the activities of the Central Bureau of the Jewish communities and with the communities themselves, finds:

1. That the communities and their central bureau serve as rallying points for enemies of the Jewish working class, and of the achievements of the October Revolution.

2. That the said communities and their central pursue an injurious policy directed at dimming the class consciousness of the Jewish working masses.

3. That forcing upon the communities the government functions in such spheres as culture and education, provides an injurious anti-

proletarian education on the growing Jewish generation.

Therefore, be it resolved by the central commissariat for Jewish national affairs:

That the central bureau of the Jewish communities and its branches on the territory of the Russian Socialist Federated Soviet Republic shall be dissolved forever.

That such funds and property shall be transferred to the local Jewish Commissariats.

That the present decree shall take effect the moment it is published in any of the official organs of the Soviet government.

For the Commissar—member of the Collegium   S. Agurski

This decree I certify

Peoples' Commissar for National Affairs   J. Stalin.[24]

This decree legalized the taking over of all the Kehilahs or Kehilah-supported institutions, the community Talmud Torahs which were wholly supported by the Kehilahs, and other types of schools which were partly subsidized by the Kehilah. However, there were stipulations. As early as August 19, 1918, the Commissariat of Jewish Affairs declared:

The Commissariat of Jewish Affairs announces that schools desiring subsidies from the Soviets, must satisfy the following conditions:

1. The language of instruction must be the native tongue (Yiddish).

2. In the first school year Hebrew is not to be taught.

3. In the second grade Hebrew should not be taught more than six hours a week.

4. In the schools that are being opened now, Hebrew is to begin with the fourth grade.

5. Religion is completely banned from the Jewish folk schools.

For the Commissar for Jewish Affairs, Sh. Tominsky.[25]

Until near the end of 1920 the Commissariat for Jewish Affairs could not enforce all its decrees and regulations, for most of the Jewish population centers were occupied by the Germans, the Polish army, or, as in the Ukraine, by various other armies. The Soviet Government consolidated the entire country at the end of 1920, and the Jewish sections of the Communist Party and the Commissariat for Jewish Affairs should have been able to begin their work. The Soviet policy had transferred all institutions to

the local Soviet authorities, however, and the Commissariat of
Jewish Affairs was nearly superfluous. The Commissariat of Jewish
Affairs was reduced to a Jewish department in the People's Com-
missariat of Nationalities in 1920, and by 1923 the Jewish Depart-
ment was reduced to one functionary. The Jewish sections of the
Communist Party were abolished seven years later.

Previously, as early as 1918–1920, existing Jewish schools had
been taken over by the local departments of education of the local
Soviet. But a Central Bureau of Jewish Education was established
at the People's Commissariat of Public Education, and this bureau
had to supervise the Jewish schools.[26]

Before the situation was stabilized, both the Commissariat for
Jewish Affairs and the Jewish sections of the Communist Party
supervised and administered Jewish affairs. A manifesto issued in
June 1918 stated:

> We, the Jewish working masses, now have an opportunity to
> shape our internal life according to our own desires and interests.
> Our comrades, the workers of other nationalities, have taken upon
> themselves the creation of a new national life on socialist founda-
> tions. In our Jewish environment, the rabbis and the rich and the
> old well-known aristocrats that are far from socialist ideals, are still
> ruling and see to it that the Jewish workers allow themselves to be
> exploited as before.
>
> Our Kehilah, our schools, all our communal institutions are serv-
> ing all except the interests of the broad masses. . . .
>
> The Jewish Commissariat's aim is to rebuild Jewish national life
> on proletarian socialist foundations. The Jewish masses now have
> full freedom to control all existing Jewish public institutions, to steer
> our public school in a socialist direction. . . .[27]

This proclamation was followed by specific instructions to the
local sections to allow that "wherever possible, the Commissariats
shall take individual institutions under their administration without
disrupting the actual functioning of the work."[28]

This directive meant the taking over of the existing schools, the
founding of new ones, and incorporating them in the local general
school system. At the same time the schools had to be subsidized
providing they fulfilled the aforementioned conditions. It also
meant the liquidation of the secular Hebrew schools, of the Tarbut
organization and of the hadorim. The secular Hebrew schools were
converted into Yiddish schools, but the hadorim were completely

liquidated. Not enough schools existed to take in the children from the ḥadorim, and a great number of children remained outside the schools. It must be pointed out, however, that compulsory education did not become effective until 1930–31.[29]

The ḥeder still existed, although it declined after the February 1917 democratic resolution; and the Jewish Communists, in their campaign against it, utilized the decree issued by the government committee for education, in September 1918:

> The Government Committee for Education, in its session August 24, 1918, discussed the petition of members of the all-Russian religious association, and it took into consideration sections 34, 35, 38 of the decree of January 23, 1918, about separation of Church and State.
>
> It therefore decrees, that for persons who have not reached the age of eighteen, no educational institutions are permitted to exist to give such religious education.[30]

On December 28, 1920, the Central Jewish Bureau of the Department of Public Education of the R.S.F.S.R. issued the following order:

> To all Education Departments, sections, instructors, about liquidating Ḥadorim and Yeshivot:
>
> The Jewish Education Department, taking into consideration the resolution of the all-Russian conference of Jewish educational workers and the reports that are being received from the various cities, has decided to start a militant campaign against the ḥadorim and yeshivot.
>
> The struggle must begin at once, even while we have no opportunity as yet to take all the children into the Soviet schools.
>
> The mere fact of destroying the ḥadorim, the Jewish Education Department considers to be a positive factor of creating and building. The children must be liberated from the terrible prison, from the full spiritual demoralization and from physical deterioration. The local education sections must consider the work of liquidating the ḥadorim for their number one aim.
>
> The work should consist of the following:
>
> 1. Agitation and enlightenment. The propaganda must be conducted among the youth. To the work must be co-opted the Communist youth, which will create an atmosphere of revolutionary struggle around the ḥeder problem against the clerical-synagogue spirit that still exists in the Jewish community. Meetings of parents

should be called where the damaging influence of the yeshivot and hadorim should be exposed. The meaning of the new socialist education in the Soviet schools should be explained. The campaign against the heder should be conducted through the press, through the living newspaper, through staged trials, and other forms of propaganda. Besides these, the educational sections must carry through preparatory steps to open, for the new school year, new schools for the children from the closed hadorim. Materials must be collected about the children in the hadorim and the yeshivot; special attention must be paid to the class-composition of the children who attend the hadorim and yeshivot; facts should be collected as to how the hadorim are maintained and who finances them. The local sections must also report how many new schools should be opened, how many teachers are needed, and what types of institutions should be opened (schools, children's homes and clubs).

Director of the Central Jewish Education Bureau

M. Levitan

Secretary, L. Sheinker[31]

Special committees of Jewish Communists were organized to liquidate the hadorim. At first, trials were staged for propaganda purposes where the heder was found guilty and the public voted to liquidate it. But soon the *melamdim* were tried by regular People's Courts and received heavy sentences for conducting a heder. Thus an official document states:

> In many localities, as for instance in Polotsk and Klintsy, the matter was tried by the People's Courts, where the aim is not an ideological struggle with the heder and those who operated it. These trials end with closing the hadorim in an administrative manner, and punishing the criminal religious functionaries and the community leaders.[32]

The biggest trial was staged in Vitebsk from the twelfth to the eighteenth of January, 1921. The experts for the prosecution had investigated the hadorim in Vitebsk, of which there were thirty-nine, containing 1,358 children. There were also forty-nine *melamdim.* Four hundred children attended a Soviet school in the morning and studied in the heder in the afternoon. The rest of the children, from eight to thirteen years old, studied only in the heder. They were divided into small groups from the ages of five to seven and thirteen to seventeen. In some of the hadorim both Russian and arithmetic were taught. Some schools were taught in Yiddish, and in some of the hadorim, Hebrew was used as the language of instruction. The conditions in the heder were reported to be unsanitary and filthy, and children were reported to be "terrorized" by beatings. The prosecutor stated:

> The result of the investigation shows that the hadorim are harmful for the spiritual and physical development of the children, they injure the soul and body of the Jewish child and bring up a generation of both physically and spiritually weak, stupefied, and cowardly people. . . .
> It should be pointed out that since religion was separated from the state, the teaching of religious subjects is prohibited ·in the schools. The neighboring nationalities have no more religious schools. Only we still have a religious school, the heder. On the basis of this, the heder is found to be fully injurious and the case is transferred to the political court.[33]

Witnesses appeared who told how detrimental the heder was, and how it ruined the lives of the children. One "expert" read from S. Maimon's autobiography describing how terrible the heder was; excerpts were also read from Moses L. Lilienblum, *Hattat Neurim* and Peretz Smolenskin's "Ha-Toe BeDarkey ha-Haim," and from Y. L. Peretz' recollections. All the excerpts painted the heder in darkest colors.[34]

There was also a defender of the heder, H. Melamed, the former State Rabbi (Kazenny Ravin). Despite the atmosphere of the trial, he delivered a scholarly and fearless defense of the heder. He challenged the prosecutor, who had based his accusations against the heder on literary, not scholarly, materials.

> Scholarly and historical materials are, in this matter, more important than the private opinions of some writers. This method shows only a one-sided picture, with the *melamed* as a dybbuk who is harming our people. One *melamed* was drawn as a character from Krafft-Ebing, and one could conclude that he is typical of all *melamdim*. The heder itself was characterized according to Voltaire's *Le Cléricalisme, voilà* Rennimi.

He disputed the prosecutor's statement that only children of the poor went to the heder. Seventeen percent of all children who attended the hadorim, according to a report of the Royal Free Economic Society, came from rich homes; and "it is difficult to believe that the percentage of well-to-do among the Jews was then larger." He defended the pedagogical abilities of the ḥeder teachers. He also pointed out that Jewish children received a superior education among Jews, than among non-Jews, and that the ḥadorim could very well be compared with the non-Jewish elementary schools.[35] National religious education is very important to the Jews; as there is no center, Jewish existence depends on "historical recollections" and the

> problem of national religious education is for us a problem of to be or not to be; therefore, these elements must occupy an important position in Jewish education—in order to implant in the child the historical-national recollections and the national thought. Here I wish to add that for every serious thinker it is not necessary to show that modern Yiddishism with its literature in Russia has very weak roots in Jewish historical thought and no connection with the general historical memories that unites us like an iron bond. The historical, national thought and the historical memories have their expression only in the Biblical and Talmudic literature, in the Jewish religion and the Hebrew language.

H. Melamed continued: "Having such bad *melamdim* [as the prosecution claims] our people are good teachers and we teach other nations. . . . It is absolutely not scientific to exchange Moses, Isaiah, and Ezra for Mendele Mokher Seforim, Peretz, and Sholem Aleichem."[36] The "Kazenny Ravin" concluded:

> The foundations of the national-religious Jewish education are: Hebrew, Bible, Agadah, and History. On the higher level the following subjects should be taught: Talmud, religious philosophy, and Jewish ethics.
> In order to provide the Jewish schools with the proper teachers, Jewish Teachers Institutes have to be established. The initiative should be left to Jewish religious associations which should be under the control of the Soviet government. Since the attendance at the government schools is obligatory, the studying at the national-religious schools should be limited to 10–12 hours per week, as in the United States.
> When teaching the Bible—certain parts can be left out or can be interpreted as symbolic.
> Until these schools can be established, the better type ḥadorim should remain.[37]

As expected, the court found the ḥeder guilty and, on January 18, 1921, issued the following judgment: "We recognize that it is vital to close the hadorim as quickly as possible and to place the children in the Yiddish schools."[38] The various trials, decrees and circulars sealed the fate of the heder. Although there were some underground hadorim here and there, the heder ceased to exist as an educational institution. The bulk of the children were admitted to the Yiddish schools. Some went to the Russian schools, and some remained outside of school as a sufficient number of schools were not available. The circular of the Jewish Bureau of the Commissariat of Education stressed that hadorim should be closed even though there were not enough schools to take in all the children.[39] In order to secure buildings for new Yiddish schools, the Jewish Communists made use of the decree which allowed the confiscation of synagogues for conversion into school buildings.

The Jewish Department of the People's Commissariat for National Affairs issued the following decree in 1922:

> Taking into consideration point six of the decree about liquidating illiteracy among the population, the organs of the People's Commissariat of Education have the right to confiscate for that purpose churches, clubs, and private houses. This decree makes it possible to make use of the synagogues. . . .
>
> We therefore advise you, together with the Jewish section of the local departments of education, to work out the proper means which are suitable to the local conditions, in order to carry through this program. We propose that at the end of each month you report to us what has been accomplished in this respect.

> Director of the Jewish Section of
> The People's Commissariat for
> National Affairs, A. Merezhin;
> Director of the Jewish Subdepartment
> of the People's Commissariat for
> Education, M. Levitan[40]

The circular was addressed to all Jewish subdepartments, departments for national affairs of the local executives of the Revolutionary Committees, and to all sections of the Communist Party.

In building the Yiddish school, the Jewish Communists utilized a decree regarding schools for national minorities issued by the People's Commissariat for Education. This decree read:

> All nationalities living in the R.S.F.S.R. have a right to organize instruction in their mother tongue. This applies to both the elementary and secondary schools.

Schools for the national minorities should be opened where there is a sufficient number of pupils of a nationality to warrant the organization of such a school. For the purpose of cultural approachability and for the development of class solidarity of the toiling people of the various nationalities, the national minorities must learn, in their schools, the language of the majority.

The schools for the national minorities are official government schools in which the same rules apply as in the unified schools.

The full direction of the schools for the national minorities is concentrated in the People's Commissariat of Education and its local and provincial sections in the localities themselves.

> Vice Commissar of People's Commissariat
> of Education, P. Mikhail Pokrovsky[41]

This decree contradicted Lenin's view that it was impossible and unnecessary to build schools for nonterritorial minorities. Lenin's theory was modified, for reasons of expediency, as a concession to the Bundist program of national cultural autonomy, opposed by both Lenin and Stalin.

It was possible for the Jewish Communists to build Yiddish schools even in cities where the Jews constituted a small minority, and for a while there were Jewish schools even in Petrograd and Moscow. The decree from the People's Commissariat of Education also incorporated the Yiddish schools into the general school system. As long as the Commissariat of Jewish Affairs existed, and the Jewish sections of the Communist Party functioned, their special education bureaus dealt with the local authorities on behalf of the Yiddish schools. When the Commissariat and, later, the Jewish sections of the Communist Party were dissolved in 1930, there were no more organized groups to intervene for the schools; only the Yiddish journalists and the Yiddish government newspapers were left.

Involvement and dealings with the local authorities wherever Yiddish schools were found was necessary from the beginning, as the authorities showed little interest in the Yiddish schools and believed them to be unnecessary.

On October 18, 1918, the Commissar of Jewish Affairs, Simon Dimanshtein, delivered a talk at a meeting of Jewish Communists:

> One of the most difficult problems is the problem of the schools. Many local soviets do not want to recognize the Yiddish schools.

They say that there should not be any separate nationality schools. This non-desirable phenomenon created many difficulties for us and we had to adopt means to put an end to this abnormal situation.[42]

Maria Y. Frumkin wrote a little later:

From all over we get reports about the difficulties that are encountered in Jewish cultural work. The decree about establishing national departments at the local boards of education are not being enforced. In the provinces, subsidies for Yiddish schools are being refused. The same boards refuse to appoint Yiddish teachers. The local officials are interested in introducing Russian as the language of instruction. Important representatives of the government are issuing special statements that employing the native tongue as the language of instruction is only a transitory medium—and the native tongue is to be used in first grade only. These tendencies of Russification are in evidence everywhere and a struggle must be carried on against them.[43]

In spite of these difficulties, a Yiddish-school system was established and developed.

NOTES

1. S. Agurski, A. Osherowitch, W. Frishman and B. Shpentser, editors, *Lenin Kegn Bund* (Lenin Against the Bund), Introduction, Belorussian Academy of Sciences, Minsk, 1935.

2. Karl Johann Kautsky (1854–1938), famous German socialist theoretician, editor, and writer. Karl Kautsky, *Are the Jews a Race?* translated from the second German edition, Jonathan Cape, London, 1926.

3. Solomon M. Schwartz, *The Jews in the Soviet Union*, Syracuse, 1951, p. 51.

4. V. I. Lenin, *Sochineniya* (Collected Works) (Russian), VI, second edition, Moscow, 1929, pp. 83 ff., quoted by Schwartz, *op. cit.*, p. 50.

5. Otto Bauer (1881–1938): Austrian socialist leader who formulated the theory of national autonomy for the national minorities of the Austro-Hungarian Empire.

6. V. I. Lenin, *Sochineniya*, XVIII, second edition, p. 141, quoted by Schwartz, *op. cit.*, p. 52.

7. Lenin, *Sochineniya*, XVII, pp. 138 ff., quoted by Schwartz, *op. cit.*, p. 53.

8. This was written in 1913, included in Lenin's *Sochineniya*, XVI, pp. 553–554, quoted from *Lenin Kegn Bund, op. cit.*, pp. 141–142.

9. Lenin, *Sochineniya*, XVII, second edition, pp. 113–115, quoted from *Lenin Kegn Bund, op. cit.*, pp. 165–166.

10. Lenin, *op. cit.*, pp. 108–109.

11. Joseph Stalin, *Marksizm, Natsionalny Vopros* (Marxism and the National Colonial Question), Moscow, 1934; Yiddish version, Moscow, 1935, pp. 33–34.

12. *Ibid.*, p. 8.

13. *Ibid.*

14. *Ibid.*, p. 39.

15. M. I. Kalinin, "Vegn der Yidisher Autonomer Gegnt" (About the Jewish Autonomous District) in *Yidn in F.S.S.R.* (Jews in U.S.S.R.), Moscow, 1935, pp. 32–33.

16. Moishe Litvakov, "Di Sovietishe Yidishe Natsie" (The Soviet Jewish Nation), *Der Emes*, Moscow, November 7, 1936.

17. A. Brakhman, "Di Bolshevistishe Partei in ir Kamf tsu Leizn di Yidishe Frage" (The Bolshevik Party in its Struggle to Solve the Jewish Problem), *For-Post*, No. 1, 1936, Birobidzhan, p. 147.

18. Declaration of the Rights of the Peoples of Russia, *Istoria Sovetskoi Konstitutsi i Dekhretakh* (History of the Soviet Constitution in Decrees), Moscow, 1936, pp. 31–32.

19. A holy language in the sense in which Hebrew was considered to be sacred.

20. S. Agurski, *Der Yidisher Arbeter in der Komunistisher Bavegung, 1917–1921* (The Jewish Worker in the Communist Movement), Minsk, 1925, pp. 44–45.

21. *Ibid.*, p. 48.

22. *Ibid.*, pp. 48–49.

23. *Ibid.*, p. 89.

24. *Ibid.*, pp. 88–89. The decree was published in *Izvestia*, June 19, 1919.

25. *Ibid.*, p. 29.

26. *A Yor Arbet fun der R.K.P. in der Yidisher Svive* (A Year's Work of the Russian Communist Party in the Jewish Environment), Moscow, 1924, p. 61.

27. Agurski, *op cit.*, pp. 21–22.

28. S. Agurski, *Di Oktober Revolutsie in Vaysrusland* (The October Revolution in Belorussia), Minsk, 1927, p. 292.

29. Schwartz, *op. cit.*, pp. 113–114.

30. L. Abram, I. Khinchon, and K. Kaplan, *Der Mishpet Ibern Kheyder* (The Trial of the Heder), Vitebsk Bureau of the Jewish Sections of the Russian Communist Party, Vitebsk, 1922, p. 87.

31. *Ibid.*, p. 88. M. Levitan was executed in 1938 as a bourgeois Jewish nationalist.

32. *Ibid.*, p. 3.

33. *Ibid.*, p. 12.

34. *Ibid.*, pp. 28 ff.

35. *Ibid.*, pp. 45–46.

36. *Ibid.*, p. 49.

37. *Ibid.*

38. *Ibid.*, p. 84.

39. See note 28.

40. *Ibid.*, p. 90. Merezhin was executed in 1938 for Jewish nationalism.

41. *Ibid.*, p. 89.

42. Simon Dimanshtein, *Baym Likht Fun Komunism* (By the Light of Communism), published by the Central Commissariat of Jewish Affairs, Moscow, 1919, pp. 283–284.

43. *Der Veker*, No. 473, Minsk, February 5, 1919.

CHAPTER 6

The Philosophy of the Soviet Jewish School

IN the first years of the Communist regime, various theories were developed concerning the goals and aims of education and the character of the schools. As early as 1919, Jewish theoreticians tried to formulate a program for the existing Yiddish schools and for those that were being organized. An official organ of the Commissariat of Education of the Belorussian and Lithuanian Soviet Republics stated in an editorial:

> The Jewish Commissariat has issued a decree that Hebrew, the Bible, and prayers are not to be taught in the first five grades. The schools are being taken over by the government and the clerical element is being removed. Only the October Revolution gave us the opportunity to create a new school. The various schools until now served the interests of the ruling classes. The ḥeder, product of the Galut, was meant for the children of the plain people. The rich and well-to-do did not send their children to the ḥeder. The Reformed ḥadorim and community Talmud Torahs were but a weak echo of the demands of the times, and they remained petrified in the obsolete forms of the old ḥadorim. The Government School for Jewish children was a child of the state bourgeois-assimilatory ideology. The only school that should serve the interests of the working class, the school that has to create a new man, is being born now, amidst

great suffering, pain, hunger, and war. The only way to build the unified secular, socialist, labor school is through the aid of the teachers, revolutionary Communists, and the toiling masses. We call upon the Communist teachers, Yiddishist teachers, who for many years have dreamt about a real Folk School, to support us in creating the new school.[1]

Although the editorial said that "Hebrew, the Bible, and prayers are not to be taught in the first five grades," the same issue carried an official decree about the school program in the newly occupied territories of Belorussia and Lithuania, which completely eliminated Hebrew, the Bible, and prayers from the school:

Decree about the Reorganization of the Schools:

About the reorganization of the schools, the Soviet of People's Commissars of Lithuania and Belorussia decrees:

All private schools are to be transferred immediately to the local agencies of the Department of Education. No tuition fee is to be charged.

All children between the ages of 8 to 17 must attend government schools. In order to carry out the separation of church and state, all instruction of religion is prohibited. All religious schools, hadorim and community Talmud Torahs are ordered to be closed and new schools will replace them.

Remark: Instruction of religion is a private matter. To force children to study religion is prohibited. Clergy and all connected with religious activity are barred from teaching positions in the schools. Instruction is to be given in the native tongue of the pupils. Besides the native tongue, the pupils should be taught one of the local languages. All schools are to be co-educational.

> W. Mizkiewicz-Kupuskas, Chairman of the Soviet of People's Commissars of Belorussia and Lithuania.
> I. Leszczinsky, Commissar of Education.
> V. Pozhelov, Director of Government Affairs.[2]

This decree was implemented by a second, issued by the executive bureau of the Soviet of Belorussia, which declared:

Conforming to the decree of the Council of People's Commissars of Lithuania and Belorussia, the languages that are recognized are: Belorussian, Russian, Yiddish, and Polish. The laws of the R.S.-F.S.R. [Russian Socialist Federal Soviet Republic] regarding the problems of education for the national minorities, and the policy of education of the Commissariat of Education, aim to give all nationalities of the republic the opportunity to receive an education in their native tongue. The executive committee does not intend to teach the children in a language with which they are not acquainted.[3]

Although the resolution stated that the languages in Belorussia are Belorussian, Russian, Yiddish, and Polish, it stressed the importance of Belorussian.

The local Yiddish schools were incorporated into the general school system. The Jewish Commissariats and, later, the local Jewish Sections of the Communist Party, initiated the process of taking over the existing Jewish schools and Sovietizing them; they also established new Jewish schools.

The Jewish Section of the Communist Party made it clear that separate Jewish schools should be organized only for those elements whose language was Yiddish, and not for Jewish children whose language was not Yiddish. Thus children of the "Subbotniks" (Russian observers of the Sabbath) should not be accepted in the Yiddish-language schools because their language was not Yiddish. It was recognized that many Jewish children were weak in both Yiddish and Russian, and therefore should be interviewed by the local school authorities to decide in which school they should be registered.[4] The Jewish Communist functionaries were as much opposed to Russian-speaking Jewish children attending the Yiddish-language schools as they were to forcing Yiddish-speaking children to attend Russian or Belorussian language schools.

The Jewish functionaries took issue with many local school boards which showed indifference or even enmity toward the Yiddish schools.[5] A report by the Central Bureau of the Jewish Sections of the Communist Party stated: "A great deal of our energy was spent to insure the rights of Yiddish education and to fight against the prejudice regarding Yiddish education, that stems from a false interpretation of internationalism."[6] The report refers to a number of instances when the local authorities closed down Yiddish kindergartens and Yiddish schools and transferred the pupils to Russian and Belorussian schools. In most cases the Jewish Bureau was successful, but sometimes the schools which were closed were not reopened. The greatest difficulties were encountered in the cities and towns in central Russia. There the Jewish population was small, there were few Yiddish-speaking Communists, and there was little or no contact at all with the Central Bureau. The report also pointed out that in some localities in the Ukraine the local authorities showed a vast indifference to the Yiddish schools; however, even there conditions were improving.[7]

The local Jewish Communist functionaries, assisted by the Central Bureau of the Jewish Section of the Communist Party and local chapters of the Jewish Commissariat, struggled to build the Yiddish-language schools while, at the same time, the Soviet government was engaged in rebuilding and expanding the school system throughout Russia. The Yiddish-language schools were designed along the same lines as the rest of the schools. By the end of 1918, the new school program was formulated and developed.[8] All the schools within the Soviet Union were under the guidance and control of the People's Commissariat of Education. Officially, the name of each school was "Integrated Soviet Labor School," abbreviated to "Soviet School," and designated by a number. All previous names of schools, such as pre-gimnazia, gimnazia, real school, or commercial high schools were abolished. The tuition-free Integrated Soviet School had two divisions, both coeducational; one, for children from ages 8–13, that is, a five-year school; and the second, for children from ages 13–17, constituting a four-year course. The teaching of religious subjects and religious customs was strictly prohibited. All teachers were appointed by the local boards of education, which were in constant touch with the Central Commissariat of Education.

The school year was divided into three periods: regular school curriculum from September 1 to June 1; school curriculum outside the classroom in the open air from June 1 to July 1; and full vacation from July 1 to September 1. All official holidays decreed by the government were celebrated at school.

The philosophy of the school favored creative work. The preparation for a useful creative labor life was the main aim of the school, for labor was highly valued. The old form of maintaining discipline was completely abolished. It was believed that this formal discipline limited the free development of the child and crippled his personality. All punishment was abolished, as well as homework and examinations, whether for school admissions or for promotion from one class to another. Instead of division into classes, wherever possible children were divided into groups according to their preparedness.

These two types of schools, the five-year elementary and the four-year secondary, together, formed an Integrated School. Originally, this Integrated School consisted of nine years, but later one year was added to create a ten-year program.

The education functionaries, in the early years of the Revolution, maintained that children should be encouraged to do independent work. Children should study those subjects which interested them most, and then should be grouped accordingly. Although the functionaries did not wish to see the children's interests become too narrow, foremost attention was paid to the subjects selected by the pupil as his main interest. It was believed that the school should strive to offer a thorough knowledge of one specialty, rather than a little knowledge about a great many things. Therefore, at a specified age, the children were divided into groups according to their interests. However, a number of subjects, which were obligatory for all pupils, formed the base that united the entire school.[9]

The purpose and the curriculum of the labor school were carefully designed to create this base:

Psychology teaches us that what remains in one's memory is that which is understood actively, through work and activity. The child thirsts for movement. He understands readily all knowledge that is presented to him through an active form, through play or work. (If properly organized, both play and work come together.) The child is usually proud of accomplishing practical work or labor that is assigned him.

The Froebel Kindergarten gives [the child] the first opportunity to do practical things, and we must demand that the same principle of doing should be maintained in all grades of the school, fitted to the age of the children and to their knowledge. It is the duty of the school to acquaint the child with all that is necessary for existence, and with those things that play the major part in life—with agriculture and industrial work—in all its phases and forms.[10]

In the first grade, the curriculum is built around manual work suited to the physical abilities of the children and according to their likes. In the second grade, industrial and agricultural work is introduced—and the pupils become acquainted with modern machines. Generally, it is not the aim of the school to prepare the children for a specific type of work, but to give them such an education that will acquaint them with the methods and forms of work—and work in the school shop, on a school model farm is important. Visits to factories are recommended.[11]

The child should deepen his knowledge through drawing, photographing, modeling, making cut-outs from cardboard, observing birds and plants. The school should also teach carpentry, construction, leatherwork, printing, ironwork. In the villages, work should be centered around farming and agriculture.

The main aim of the elementary school curriculum should be to fuse all the elements together, and acquaint the child, through work and doing, with both the surrounding nature and with the social environment. Thus playing, talks, and walks give the child material for collective and individual thought and activity. The function of the teacher should be to direct and systematize the child's eagerness and curiosity, without force, and thus achieve the best results.

In the higher grades, the curriculum should include the teaching of specific subjects and imparting of knowledge. The pupils take up the study of a "specific cultural subject, which they consider as a product both of nature and of work." In studying this subject, the teachers take up some elements of science, showing the influence and accomplishments of science. Then the pupils, through independent activity, take up the history and evolution of the labor process, and history of the development of society. The evolution of man, and the development of work should be taught not only through telling and reading, but through the reconstruction of primitive society, through projects. In the upper grades, courses in social studies and economics should be given, and also a full understanding of production, capital and labor, socialism and capitalism. History, with an economic interpretation, in depth, should be taught, and the pupils should be encouraged to do independent research, prepare papers, and give talks to the class. In the higher classes of the elementary school, and especially in the secondary school, systematic instruction should be given in language, mathematics, geography, history, biology, physics, chemistry, and foreign languages.[12]

But all subjects taken up in school must be connected with the life and work of the environment. The curriculum should be unified and adjusted to the environment. The work that the pupils do must not be a plaything, but real creative work, and the pupils should maintain close ties with the economic and industrial life of the community. Pupils should spend some time at the library, at the laboratory, in visits to industrial plants and museums of industry, and should at all times be encouraged to do independent work.

Drawing, sculpture, and music should form an important element of the school curriculum, as should the pupils' participation in gymnastics, choral singing and acting in school plays.

The theoreticians of education maintained that the curriculum should include esthetic education because the aim of education, of science, and of work was the joy of living, and the joy of creativity, and the feeling of accomplishment.[13]

Special attention was paid to the student as an individual. The teacher observed the character and interests of each pupil, and included their personal needs with the general instruction in the school. The school intended to free the children from egoism, to train them to work collectively and to develop a feeling for collective action. Formerly, individualized instruction was for the purpose of enabling the individual to compete for first place. However, socialist education strove to create "psychic collectives," and was proud of the fact that it did not hinder, but encouraged the development of talented individuals. The children, in preparation for a socialist society, had to learn first to become part of the school. School councils were organized and the pupils elected their own officers.[14] The Soviet school, completely secular, aimed at creating a school collective, united through a healthy group feeling. Thus, the students would identify themselves as an important part of the collective.[15]

The ideologists of education were no doubt influenced by John Dewey,[16] but they adjusted his ideas to conform with the Communist program and with the aims of the Soviet government. To Dewey's ideas were added those of a socialist school, formulated by the leading Communist, Nadezhda Krupskaya (Mrs. Lenin). She stated in her essay, "Regarding the Problem of the Socialist School,"[17] that schools in the capitalist countries implanted in the children the morals of the bourgeoisie. The eradication of class consciousness made the masses an obedient herd to be dominated and ruled by the bourgeoisie.[18] The aim of education in the capitalist countries, continued Krupskaya, was to train a bureaucracy to help the ruling classes govern. The schools destroyed all potentialities for independent thinking. She said the bourgeois public school is a tool to enslave the working people by separating them from the living environment, and from productive labor.

After criticizing the schools of former times, N. Krupskaya described the proposed program for the new Soviet school. It should first ensure the physical development of the child. Then the child should be trained to observe things, through creative play. The child should have the opportunity to express himself in pictures, and therefore should be provided with materials for drawing, painting, and sculpting, and with cardboard for cutting into shapes. The child should have full freedom to express his creative personality. The school should give each child the opportunity to develop his social instincts and interests in the lives of other people.

The school should demonstrate that the basis of co-living and co-existence is toil and labor, and should awaken in the child the joy of creative productive labor; the child should be a useful member of the entire community. Children should be trained to work collectively in preparation for adulthood. A child trained to work appreciates and estimates his own capabilities, and also learns his limitations. Work and play in common among his peers trains the child to develop moral responsibility. The elementary school must prepare the child to develop a desire for productive and useful work, train him to observe and to imitate work, and teach him to work with a group.

In the secondary school, training was systematized. Pupils learned the construction of society, and studied the different branches of science. The pupil in the secondary school acquired and analyzed a great many facts from different perspectives and by various methods. He developed a view of the world, a certain attitude. N. Krupskaya believed that the Socialist School should develop the child fully and not suppress his individuality. Individuality should be expressed in useful and purposeful work, and it was the responsibility of the school to develop the productive potentialities of the children. N. Krupskaya planned for the schools to have machine shops and gardens, where it would be shown that learning, interrelated with labor, produced results which were useful to both the individual and society. But, she continued, only in a socialist society, such as existed in Russia, where there was a fair apportionment of labor, could such a school exist. The school must produce a new man, who understands the importance of labor, and works with enthusiasm, and who can adjust to various and constantly changing forms and means of production. This was the purpose of the new school.[19]

N. Krupskaya stressed the importance of a secular school for, just as the government separated church and state, so also should the school system. No representatives of any religion should be able to influence the young child. The rights of the child must be protected and guaranteed. Children should not be exploited by hard labor, nor should they be exploited by the various religious representatives. "The weak creatures," as Krupskaya called the children, must be guarded against the religious functionaries who would damage their souls. As a communist ideologist, Krupskaya developed the theory that in the bourgeois schools, a priest, a minister, or a rabbi taught the children to be obedient servants of an unknown God. Children were trained in the morality of servants and slaves, to love all, including exploiters, and not to resist evil, the morality of both exploiters and obedient slaves. For two thousand years Christianity preached love and forgiveness, and the world was drenched in blood. Religious morality was decidedly against the best interests of the working people. Therefore, children should not be taught anything, including the Bible, which is contradicted by science and history.[20] N. Krupskaya's writings were not merely an author's articles and essays, but were officially inspired documents that formulated a program for the school system; these programs were adopted by all schools in the Soviet Union.

All the Yiddish-language schools in existence, those formerly for refugee children, the former government Jewish schools, community Talmud Torahs, and Tarbut schools (elementary and secondary schools where the language of instruction was Hebrew and the philosophy was Zionism), and the newly organized schools had to adjust to the new type of schools called either work schools, unified schools or elementary or secondary work schools.[21] The Jewish Communist functionaries were to adjust the curriculum, eliminate all Jewish and Yiddishist elements, and make sure that the schools fit in with the official Communist philosophy of education. It is important to know Lenin's views on pedagogy and the aims of the Soviet school for they were incorporated into the school curriculum.

The Soviet pedagogues diligently studied the works of Lenin and quoted anything that could be classified as guidance in formulating the aims and curriculum of the Soviet school. Lenin, of course, believed that all education should first serve the acquisition of power by the Communist Party; and that once power was acquired, education should serve the new state. Lenin declared:

> The old school proclaimed that it strove to produce a fully developed and educated personality, through teaching sciences generally. We know this is a false assumption [about developing a full personality] because the entire society is based on class divisions, on

those exploited and on those who exploit. It is natural that the old
school was permeated with the spirit of class divisions, and that this
school imparted knowledge to the children of the bourgeoisie. Every
word of the school was falsified in the interests of the bourgeoisie.[22]

Lenin further said that in the activities of the Communist Party,

There is an element of pedagogy, the wage-earning classes must
be educated and prepared to become fighters for the liberation of
the entire human race. . . . The new rising generations must be
taught in such a way that they should be brought to the ideas of
socialism. We must not convert our teaching into a dry dogma, we
must teach [them] not only through a textbook—but through participation in the daily struggle of the proletariat.[23]

Lenin also declared openly that the "proletariat," which would take
over the old capitalist society, must also take over the education
of the new generations which would build the socialist society and
accomplish the aim of the new regime:

In the field of public education the Communist Party strives to
convert the school, which was a tool of the ruling capitalist class,
into an arm to completely destroy the class society and into a means
of rebuilding the old society into a new communist society.[24]

Lenin stressed the point that "only on the foundation of modern
education can the communist society be built, and if the working
class will not possess the new education, communism will remain
only a wish."[25] Lenin further stated:

We must not take from the old school that element with which
the memory of the children was overloaded; we must not give them
information that is 90 percent not essential, and the 10 percent
which is, is given in a crippled fashion. But that does not mean that
we must limit ourselves to communist slogans. This way, communism will not be established. One becomes a communist only
when one enriches his memory with knowledge and with knowing
all the riches that humanity has acquired and developed. We must
not only commit to memory, but we must develop and fill the memory of each pupil with knowledge of facts. Communism would be
converted into an emptiness, into a blank sign, if in the mind all the
facts and knowledge would not become systematized and formulated.[26]

Lenin formulated a program for the school which incorporated
both science and the humanities. A knowledge of electricity and

its application as power in industry, chemistry and its practical application, and the basic facts about agriculture were to be taught. Children should also receive instruction in Communism, general history, history of revolutions, geography, and literature. Lenin stressed the importance of introducing a work bench in each school. Laboratories and the school workshop occupied an important place in the curriculum. The pupils of the higher grades of the secondary schools worked part of the time in the factories to receive a first-hand acquaintance with methods of production, and factory organization. They regularly visited and learned about hydroelectric stations. The pupils also visited farms to gather all available data on agricultural production.[27]

Lenin's and N. Krupskaya's views about the character of the school, its purpose and aims, were incorporated into the school programs and curriculum. All schools, including the Jewish schools, were built around the same program. If the Russian schools eliminated all religious instruction and all bourgeois elements, the Jewish schools had to follow by eliminating not only Hebrew and religion, but all vestiges of Jewish nationalism, including Yiddishism and Folkism.

As early as 1921, the Education Bureau of the Jewish Section of the Communist Party took up the problem of the Jewish content of the Yiddish-language schools. A report published in August 1921, stated:

Jewish educational work was, until recently, politically and ideologically on a very low plane. In our educational institutions, the spirit of Yiddishism and of petit-bourgeois Folkism (Populism) reigned. The Jewish educational officials and the teachers were, in most cases, far from communism, and neither the teacher nor the official had any political aims. The children were, therefore, brought up mainly on such works of Yiddish literature that should not occupy any position in the Communist school.

The so-called Jewish studies, Jewish history and other subjects, were taught in a spirit of nationalism without the proper Marxist orientation. The International proletarian holidays occupied a small place, while the Jewish national holidays were cultivated—and in a very Jewish spirit. Little time and attention was devoted to political education. No struggle was conducted against religious moods, feelings, and views of the pupils.

The Central Jewish Education Bureau acted upon this, by specific instructions—and these instructions brought concrete results. The local education bureaus of the Jewish Sections of the Communist Party realized the necessity of bringing about radical changes in the work. Thus, the internationalist communist element in education gradually achieved its proper place both in the schools and in the institutions for homeless children. The proletarian holidays began to compete with the national holidays. In many places and localities international children's festivals are being arranged.

Since the local Party Sections paid little attention to political activity at the Jewish educational institutions, and have not conducted any Communist work among the teachers and have not organized any Communist cells among the students of the pedagogical courses, the Central Education Bureau has sent reminders to the local bureaus about the necessary changes, and about stressing the necessity for political education.

The problem of Communist and political education occupies an important position in the special summer courses that were conducted for teachers and educational functionaries.

In the last year, the spirit of Yiddishism in our schools has been replaced with the spirit of communism. The eradication of petit-bourgeois, nationalistic, and clerical tendencies among children and teachers has been completed. The problem of introducing Yiddish as the language of instruction is not being considered as a value in itself—but as a natural continuation of the Communist education of the Jewish masses.

The educational work is no longer of an abstract nature, but is fitted to the needs of the Jewish proletarian masses. An important position in the Jewish schools is now occupied by both political and technical education, an education that is directly related to the working class and to the needs of the Soviet government.[28]

From this and other similar statements it became clear that the Jewish school was really a Soviet school, using the Yiddish language as the language of instruction. Although Yiddish and Yiddish literature were only taught as special subjects, they gave some Jewish content to the school. These two subjects were taught from a narrow party point of view but nevertheless they had a nationalizing effect and made the pupils conscious of their Jewishness. The majority of the Jewish children who did not attend the Jewish schools became more estranged from Jewish life than those who did attend.

The Jewish Communists were aware of the fact that no matter how much the Jewish schools were purged of all Jewish elements, the teaching of Yiddish literature had a Jewish value. They therefore stressed that "Jewish educational work has to do only with those Jewish people who speak Yiddish," and that the school should not teach Yiddish and Yiddish literature to those who did not speak the language.[29] The Central Bureau of the Jewish Section of the Communist Party discussed whether or not educational work should be carried out to Yiddishize the mountain Jews of the Caucasus, who spoke no Yiddish. Although some officials were in favor, the Jewish Bureau abandoned the attempt.[30]

In the first few years after the Communist seizure of power, there was general confusion and overlapping of work. The Yiddish schools were administered at the local level either by the local branch of the Jewish Section of the Communist Party, or by the local branch of the Jewish Commissariat. But by 1921, a Jewish Bureau, directed by M. Levitan, was established at the Central Department of Education. In his report about the work accomplished to the middle of August 1921, Levitan stated that the Central Jewish Education Bureau had become part of the Commissariat of Education, and had made contacts with the local schools and school functionaries. Special instructors were trained to visit the local schools and to direct their activities. An agency was established in Moscow to train teachers and administrators for the schools. The Central Bureau also transferred many Jewish teachers from Russian to Yiddish schools and stopped the transfer of teachers from the Jewish schools to Russian and other language schools. The Bureau took upon itself the provision of textbooks for the Jewish schools.

The Bureau also conducted a propaganda campaign among the local school authorities who still retained some tendencies toward Russification, and had obstructed the growth of the Yiddish schools. At the same time, the Central Bureau conducted a successful campaign against Yiddishist tendencies, for the school was only for those Jewish children whose mother tongue was Yiddish.

The Central Bureau also conducted a successful campaign for closing all the remaining hadorim and yeshivot. The Bureau succeeded in incorporating the Yiddish schools in the regular school system and provided that its budget should be covered by the general school board.[31]

The first all-Russian convention of Jewish educators, held in Moscow July 1920, issued directives to the Jewish Bureau of the Commissariat of Education. This cultural convention was attended by two hundred delegates, of whom three-quarters were Communists. The convention received directives from the third all-Russian conference of the Jewish Sections of the Communist Party, which was held in Moscow from July 4th to 10th, 1920. The Jewish Communist conference was attended by sixty-four delegates with voting privileges, and by twenty-two delegates who had only advisory rights. The majority of the delegates had joined the Jewish Sections of the Communist Party in 1919. Among them were thirty-four former Bundists, eleven former members of the United Jewish Socialist Labor Party (Zionists-Socialists), seven former Poale Zionists (Labor Zionists), two former Mensheviks, and one former anarchist. The following directives were sent to the first conference of educators, held immediately after the conference of the Jewish Communists:

The chief aim of all the cultural and educational work among the Jewish population is to develop among the Jewish people a communist ideology, to deepen their class consciousness, to strengthen the struggle of the Jewish proletariat and to prepare it for the rebuilding of society.

Therefore, the conference recommends that the Jewish educational organizations free themselves of those cultural traditions that are a result of a different epoch and do not express the needs of the present epoch of the universal proletarian revolution. The activity and work of the technical organizations should be the introduction of proletarian culture in all fields of education.[32]

This first convention of the Jewish educators and cultural functionaries accepted the directives of the Jewish Sections of the Communist Party and adopted resolutions whose text incorporated these directives:

The Soviet Government and Jewish Education
The convention affirms that since the October revolution, a significant number of educational institutions have been established, and a foundation has been laid for a Jewish educational apparatus. This all was made possible due to the accomplishments of the October Revolution, and to the educational policy of the Soviet Government, and to the struggle of those parts of the Jewish workers that have actually carried through the principles of the proletarian dictatorship among the Jews.

Jewish Councils for People's Education
In order that the work should be continued successfully, councils for Jewish people's education should be organized.

The first step to organize such councils is to call town, provincial, and state [guberniya] conferences, the delegates being selected through the workers' organizations. Broader masses should be mobilized for cultural work and from these delegates new groups of educational functionaries will eventually develop.

In order to create the necessary atmosphere of proletarian participation around the Jewish educational institutions immediately and in order to awaken both their initiative and activity, the Jewish Communists should be co-opted to the leadership of all cultural and educational organizations, and these Jewish Communists should organize the dictatorship of the proletariat in the cultural work.

The Yiddish School

Due to many difficulties and obstructions, some educational functionaries began to doubt the viability of the work school. The conference warns against this tendency. Experience has shown that amidst the most difficult conditions, even in a poor Yiddish-school atmosphere, it is possible to lay the foundation for this type of school, which has as its main principles collective, organized labor, self-management, direct contact with surrounding life, organic unity between physical and spiritual labor, and education for a communist society.

As for the curriculum, the convention finds it once more necessary to condemn sharply the longing for the old school, with its hourly division from bell to bell with its many subjects. The curriculum should be grouped around two main centers: nature and man. The school is being built along the principles of work and activity according to a wide plan fitted to the conditions of the specific place and of the school, and according to the needs of the children.

The convention adopted a resolution to liquidate illiteracy among Jewish adults and to organize trade courses to improve the labor productivity of the Jewish workers. The convention also adopted a resolution to reform Yiddish spelling; the phonetic principle must be adopted, but the alphabet should not be changed. The Hebrew element had to be naturalized and spelled according to the rules of Yiddish spelling.[33]

The first resolution that was quoted stated that "since the October Revolution a significant number of educational institutions have been established." It is true that some new schools were founded, but most of the schools were simply taken over, such as the Yiddish schools for refugee children, the former Russian-language Jewish schools and the former Hebrew Tarbut schools. Moreover, the trade schools that previously belonged to the ORT organization (from the Russian *Obshchestvo Remeslenogo Truda,* a central agency which developed trade schools and agriculture for Jews) were incorporated into the regular school system. The Jewish Communists took over the various existing Jewish schools, extended, Sovietized and Yiddishized them. The conference took credit for a school system which, in fact, it did not establish.[34] Jewish councils for "people's" education, which the resolution called for, never materialized. The Jewish schools were incorporated into the local school system, the Central Jewish Bureau of the People's Commissariat of Education, and the Bureau of Education of the Jewish Section of the Communist Party helped in some degree to supervise those schools. But bureaus were abolished with the liquidation of the Jewish Section of the Communist Party in 1930.

NOTES

1. Editorial in *Folksbildung,* No. 2, Vilna, April 4, 1919, p. 2.
2. *Ibid.,* p. 32.
3. *Tsum XV Yortog fun der Oktiaber Revolutsie, Sotsial-Economisher Zamlbukh,* Minsk, 1932, pp. 150–151.
4. *Partei-Materialn* (Party Materials) of the Central Bureau of the Jewish Sections of the Russian Communist Party, No. 5, August 1921, p. 34.
5. *Ibid.,* p. 31.
6. *Ibid.*
7. *Ibid.,* p. 32.
8. See note 9 for source.
9. S. Genrikh, "Di Kultur Oiftuen fun der Ruslendisher Ratn Republik" (The Cultural Accomplishments of the Russian Soviet Republic), in *Di Naye Velt,* No. 1–2, January–February 1919, Vilna, pp. 90 f.
10. *Ibid.,* p. 94.
11. *Ibid.*
12. *Ibid.,* p. 96.
13. *Ibid.,* p. 97.
14. *Ibid.*
15. *Ibid.,* p. 98.
16. William Heard Kilpatrick, *Philosophy of Education,* New York, 1951; "Pavlov's Teachers' Training Schools," George L. Kline, editor, *Soviet Education,* London, 1957, pp. 121 ff; George S. Counts, *The Challenge of Soviet Education,* New York, 1957, pp. 60–61, pp. 82–95; Kopelev, F. F., *Sovietskaia Shkola v Period Sotsialistiheskoy Industrializatsia* (The Soviet School in the Period of Socialist Industrialization), Moscow, 1959, pp. 90 ff; B. Shevkin, *Pedagogika Dzhan Dewey na Sluzhbe Sovremenoi Amerikanskoi Reaktsi* (The

Pedagogy of John Dewey in Service of Contemporary American Reaction), Moscow, 1952. P. K. Groser, *Nighlizma Dzhana Dewey* (The Nihilism of John Dewey), Moscow, 1958.

17. *Kultur Fragn, An Almanac,* Vol. I, edited by N. Bukhbinder, Z. Greenberg and S. Dimanshtein, Petersburg, 1918.

18. *Ibid.,* p. 24.

19. *Ibid.,* pp. 25 ff.

20. *Ibid.,* pp. 33–36.

21. Abraham Golomb, *A Halber Yorhundert Yidishe Dertsiung* (Half A Century of Jewish Education), Rio de Janeiro, 1957, pp. 99 ff., 111 ff.

22. Quoted from G. Gorokhov, *Lenin Vegn Frages fun Pedagogie un Shul Boyung* (Lenin on Problems of Pedagogy and School Development), Kiev, 1934, p. 17. Original: Lenin, *Sochineniya* (Collected Works), Vol. 30, second edition, pp. 405 f.

23. Gorokhov, *ibid.,* p. 21. Lenin, Vol. 8, pp. 308–309.

24. Gorokhov, *ibid.,* p. 26. Lenin, Vol. 23, p. 66.

25. Gorokhov, *ibid.,* p. 27. Lenin, Vol. 30, p. 409.

26. Gorokhov, *ibid.,* pp. 28, 29. Lenin, Vol. 30, p. 407.

27. Gorokhov, *ibid.,* p. 43. Lenin, Vol. 30, pp. 418–419.

28. *Partei Materialn* (Party Materials) of the Central Bureau of the Jewish Sections of the Communist Party, No. 5, August 1921, pp. 32–33.

29. *A Yor Arbet* (A New Year's Work of the Russian Communist Party in the Jewish Environment), Moscow, 1924, p. 50. See also Eliahu Tcherikower, *Kumunistishe Kemfer fun Hebreish in Turkestan* (Communist Fighters for Hebrew in Turkestan), in *In Der Tekufe fun Revolutsie* (In the Revolutionary Period), Vol. I, Berlin, 1924, pp. 356–366. See also, Emanuel Saegaller, "Anthropology in Miniature—A Note on the Jews of Soviet Georgia (Gruzia)," *Jewish Social Studies,* Vol. XXVI, No. 4, October 1964, pp. 195 ff.

30. *Partei Yedies,* No. 5, August 1921, p. 13.

31. M. Levitan, "Report of the Activities of the Central Jewish Bureau of the Nationalities Council of the People's Commissariat of Education, in *Yedies Partei Materialn,* No. 5, August 1921, pp. 29 ff.

32. *Yedies Partei Materialn* of the Central Bureau of the Jewish Section of the Central Committee of the All-Russian Communist Party, No. 1, October 1920, p. 25.

33. *Yedies, ibid.,* pp. 25–26.

34. *Yedies Partei Materialn, op. cit.,* No. 5, August 1921, p. 36.

CHAPTER 7

The Development of the Yiddish School

THE split of the Russian Social Democratic Party into Bolshevik and Menshevik factions occurred at the third congress, held in London, in 1903. These two factions developed later into separate Social Democratic parties, the Bolshevik and the Menshevik parties. The Jewish Labor Bund was an autonomous Menshevik party within the Russian Social Democratic Party.

There were some Jews among the Bolsheviks, but the Jewish Bolsheviks were of the type of Grigori Zinoviev, Leo Kamenev and Maxim Litvinov,[1] assimilated Russian-speaking people, who showed no interest in Jewishness and the Jews. Among the leading Bolsheviks, or Communists, there was only one person, Simon Dimanshtein, who had had a Jewish education and was interested in doing work among the Jewish workers in Russia. In 1905, Dimanshtein and a few Yiddish-speaking Communists published a Yiddish translation of the *Report of the Third Congress of the Russian Social Democratic Labor Party*.[2] However, Bolshevism found very little response among the Jewish workers and intellectuals. Most of the politically inclined Jews belonged to the various Jewish political parties, such as the Bund, the Poale Zion, the People's Party, and the Jewish Socialist Party.

After the Communists seized power in November 1917, many Jews joined the Communist Party, as individuals, but the bulk of the membership consisted of former Bundists, Poale Zionists, Territorialists. These parties disintegrated after the Communists seized power, and many of the active members joined the newly formed Jewish sections of the Communist Party.[3] Actually, the members of the Jewish sections of the Communist Party belonged both to the general all-Russian Communist Party and to the Jewish sections of the party. The Jewish sections carried out the revolution among the Jews, and supervised the development and maintenance of the Yiddish-language schools.[4]

As noted earlier, the report of the third all-Russian Conference of the Jewish sections of the Communist Party stated that most of the section members had joined the party in 1919, nearly all of them having formerly been Bundists, Poale Zionists, and Socialist Territorialists.[5] These new Communists were not only Yiddish-speaking Communists, they were Jews interested in Jewishness, in Jewish culture and the existence of the Jewish people. They all knew Lenin's and Stalin's views on the Jewish problem, and they knew that both men believed the only solution for the Jewish problem to be total assimilation. However, the new Jewish Communists saw possibilities for Jewish work in the recently established Commissariat for Nationalities and in the post of Commissar for Jewish Affairs.[6] The Communist rulers realized that there were millions of Yiddish-speaking Jews in Russia who were concentrated in many nearly all-Jewish towns and cities and, for reasons of expediency, they allowed cultural and educational work to be carried on among the people until the population would become integrated and assimilated. The Jewish Communists took over the various existing Jewish schools, Sovietized them, and expanded the school system.

The Jewish Communists made certain that the declaration dealing with full equality of languages was observed by the government officials and that, in the various republics, the schools in the languages of the minority would have opportunities equal to those of the majority. In the Republics of the Ukraine and in Belorussia, the Jewish Communists fought against Russification and for the rights of Yiddish and the Yiddish school.[7] Those Communists who were active in the Jewish sections criticized the functionaries who compromised in favor of Russian or Ukrainian and neglected cul-

tural and educational work in Yiddish. At the same time they
warned against doing work in Yiddish among Jews who did not
speak the language.[8] In their anxiety to help both the Ukrainians
and Belorussians achieve the full hegemony of their languages, the
Central Bureau of the Jewish Sections of the Communist Party in
1932 directed that in each republic the local language should be
taught as a separate subject in the Yiddish schools.[9]

The Jewish Communists also paid attention to the development
of the Yiddish school system. A leading Jewish Communist, Esther
Frumkin, complained that the Jewish sections often neglected all
work in favor of work for the Yiddish school.[10] But in the same
report which Esther Frumkin delivered in 1923, she emphasized
that:

> It is necessary to work systematically to see that the Jewish work-
> ers and toilers should participate actively in the building of the Yid-
> dish school, to popularize the principles of proletarian education
> through lectures, exhibits and by calling, often, meetings of the par-
> ents.[11]

Maria Frumkin (Esther), the former Bundist, who formulated the
necessity of a Yiddish Folk School as early as 1909, continued, as
a Communist, to work for the Soviet Yiddish school. She stressed
the importance of carrying on Yiddish propaganda for Jewish
Communism. The Jewish Communist functionaries who knew Yiddish, she felt, should help in the establishment of special schools
for adults who were illiterate, to help end illiteracy. She urged that
propaganda be carried on in Yiddish, and that Lenin's works be
published immediately in Yiddish. She warned that Communist
propaganda work should also be carried on among the teachers in
the Yiddish schools. Frumkin said: "It is necessary at the same
time to be on the lookout for the emergence of nationalistic, Yiddishist deviations, and not to permit ideologies which are foreign
to the proletariat in the Yiddish school."[12]

M. Levitan, a leader of the Jewish section and head of the
Bureau of Education of the Jewish Sections of the Communist
Party, submitted a report to the conference of the Jewish Sections
that was held in 1923, covering the entire period to that date.
Among the important points that he stressed concerning cultural
activities were: the incorporation of the Jewish educational institutions, and the local bureaus that supervised them, in the general

school system; the fact that general educational institutions paid more attention to the Yiddish schools, and recognized their importance.

By this year, 1923, the existence of the Yiddish school has been strengthened. Some schools have been provided with better buildings, many buildings were repaired and schools were provided with various instruments. The Yiddish language has been introduced as the language of instruction in all grades of Jewish educational institutions. Besides the four-year schools, there are now both seven- and nine-year schools.

Pedagogy and instruction have been improved, and the Jewish schools are among the best in the various districts. In most of the schools the Sabbath and Jewish religious holidays have been abolished as days of rest. The Jewish schools have liberated themselves from every form of masked religious education. The use of literary material that contains nationalistic and petit-bourgeois moods has been done away with. The internationalist element has been strengthened. The political education of the pupils has been improved, in the direction of communist ideology. The work of the Pioneers and the Young Communist League has a proper place in the schools. The atheistic propaganda among the pupils has made progress, and the pupils are taking part in antireligious demonstrations. The Jewish Soviet school has become a revolutionary factor in the Jewish milieu.

The Jewish teaching profession has been purged of casual elements, those who cannot or who will not adjust themselves, pedagogically and politically, to the Soviet school; great work has been done to reorient the teachers.

A foundation has been laid for the systematic administration, supervision and direction of the Jewish schools. New textbooks that fit the schools have been prepared.

Teachers' training institutes were organized and now there are eight such seminaries. Among the students there are a great many Communists and members of the Young Communist League.

All hadorim and yeshivot have been liquidated throughout the Soviet Union. In connection with the liquidation of these institutions, propaganda campaigns have succeeded in accomplishing their aim and the Jewish masses look with contempt on the clergy. We have also prevented any hadorim from emerging in the form of private instruction. The attempt of the Jewish bourgeoisie to smuggle through the instruction of Hebrew in the Jewish schools has been suppressed. The Leningrad Institute for Higher Jewish Studies has been reorganized and it is now a Soviet institution. We have not permitted the revival of the old Jewish bourgeois educational associations.

We have succeeded in clarifying the main principles of the Soviet Jewish cultural work for the Jewish toiling masses and we fought the petit-bourgeois prejudices against this cultural construction. At the same time it must be pointed out that although we have accomplished much, we are still behind in our work. Success has been achieved due to the material aid of the Jewish social organizations [the Jewish Social Committee], but these funds have now been exhausted. The educational institutions with Yiddish as the language of instruction that serve the Yiddish-speaking population are still too few. The elementary schools, for example, embrace not more than 20 or 25 percent of all Yiddish-speaking children.[13]

M. Levitan further stressed that the shortcomings in Jewish educational work were due to tendencies of Russification, and to the indifference many local educational boards or bureaus showed to the Yiddish school. Various local school boards closed down the Jewish bureaus, or reduced their personnel, and the local boards of education granted inadequate funds for the Yiddish-language schools. Lack of coordination between the various republics had a negative influence on the field of Jewish educational work. But Levitan further pointed out in his report that the Central Bureau of Jewish Education of the Jewish Sections of the Communist Party had succeeded in its struggle to have the existing Jewish schools retained as part of each local school system with sufficient funds to maintain them. M. Levitan called for a strict enforcement of the principle that children should receive their education in their mother tongue. Beginning in 1924, all schools with a large proportion of Yiddish-speaking pupils, including trade schools, should be Yiddishized, or special Yiddish classes should be established. At the beginning of the new term, the native language of each child should be determined, and the children should be assigned according to the schools employing that language as the language of instruction. The assignment of the children to the specific-language schools should be done after the proper propaganda campaign. At the same time, every tendency of nationalism should be eliminated.

In accordance with the plan that all children receive compulsory education, the Jewish children who, at that time, did not attend any school should be provided with schooling. Steps should be taken to insure that the entire budget of the Yiddish-language

schools should be included in the local school budgets.
M. Levitan suggested that those Jewish teachers who knew
Yiddish and taught in Russian schools, should be transferred to the
growing number of Yiddish schools where there was a shortage of
teachers. He also recommended that a teachers' seminary be established in Moscow to serve the entire Soviet Union. In his fight
against nationalism, Levitan believed that more Jewish Communists who knew Yiddish should be appointed as inspectors in the
schools and teachers' seminaries. He concluded his report by
reiterating that all Yiddish-language schools were for Yiddish-
speaking Jews only, those whose native tongue was Yiddish, and
not for those Jews who spoke Russian or any other language.[14]

M. Levitan delivered his report to the all-Union conference of
the Jewish Sections of the Communist Party, April 4, 1924. After-
wards, the conference adopted a resolution approving it and
declared that it "be resolved to conduct a systematic activity in
transferring all educational institutions to the use of Yiddish as
the language of instruction." The conference also adopted a resolution that the Belorussian language should be taught in the Yiddish
schools in Belorussia, and Ukrainian in the Ukraine.[15]

The Jewish Sections of the Communist Party in the Ukraine held
a conference in October 1925. At that time the Ukraine was
experiencing a process of Ukrainization, in which Russian was
being pushed out and replaced by the Ukrainian language. This
created an opportunity for Yiddish and an increase in the number
of Yiddish schools and pupils. Jewish parents were anxious to
send their children into Russian-language schools, but when the
choice was limited to Ukrainian or Yiddish schools, the parents
grudgingly registered their children in the Yiddish schools.

A representative of the Central Committee of the Communist
Party and of the government of the Ukrainian Socialist Soviet
Republic, Popov, greeted this conference of the Jewish Sections
of the Communist Party. He spoke about the Ukrainization and,
also, about the process of Yiddishization in the Ukraine. The
conference, after Popov's speech, adopted the following resolution:

> The conference maintains that the Ukrainization which is being
> carried out resolutely through the party, leads to a greater and
> stronger unity between the majority of the toiling population in the
> Ukraine, and the party and the Soviet government; that the workers
> and toilers of all nationalities in the Ukraine, among them also the

Jewish, are interested in the urgent achievement of this task. A hard
struggle has to be conducted against the Russification trends that
are still prevalent among some workers, including Jewish, both in
regard to Ukrainization and Yiddishization. In this connection, the
conference stresses that the party must not shut its eyes to the dan-
ger of possible nationalistic deviations regarding the problem of the
national policy. The conference remarks with satisfaction that the
work among the national minorities, including the Jewish minority,
has improved, but it maintains that there is more to be accomplished among the Jews.

In order to strengthen the work among the Jewish toiling masses,
it is necessary to introduce Yiddish as the official language in the
trade unions, in the cells of the Communist Party and in the organizations of the Young Communist League, where the Jews constitute
a majority. Party propaganda and cultural work in Yiddish must
be increased. The Jewish Sections of the Communist Party need the
capable functionaries who now do general party work. The conference also recommends publishing more books in Yiddish and
organizing local Jewish Soviets and adjusting the government apparatus to serve the Jewish population in its native language.[16]

The conference also heard a talk by M. Levitan, who spoke of
the urgency of adopting Yiddish as the language in all Jewish
unions, clubs, local Soviet party organizations and in all educational
work carried on among Jews.[17]

To the published text of the speeches and resolutions was added
a supplement with directives by the Workers' and Peasants' Inspection Committee of the Central Committee of the Communist Party.
Among the directives was one which stated:

> The People's Commissariat of Education must pay special atten-
> tion in order to register the children of the national minorities in the
> mass-school and to broaden the scope of the school system of the
> national minorities, where the given national minority constitutes a
> majority in the locality.

The same Workers' and Peasants' Inspection Committee reiterated
that all private religious schools and hadorim should be absolutely
prohibited.[18]

In the years between 1917 and 1932, the Yiddish schools showed
a great growth and expansion. Belorussia and the Ukraine, where
nearly all Soviet Yiddish schools functioned, were occupied by
various non-Soviet occupation forces from 1918 to 1920 with the
result that, until the end of 1920, school development was irregular

and uneven. Thus some of the Yiddish schools that were organized under the Soviet rule early in 1919, became religious schools when Belorussia was occupied by the Polish army.[19] But a regular development was marked with the stabilization of the Soviet regime, both in Belorussia and the Ukraine at the end of 1920 and the beginning of 1921.

Here it should be stressed that the bases for the Soviet Yiddish schools were the Yiddish refugee schools founded under the Tsarist regime in 1915–1916; the various Russian-language Jewish schools, both government and private; and the former Hebrew Tarbut schools and community Talmud Torahs. The various Soviet Jewish writers who wrote about the development of the Soviet Yiddish school ignored the facts and claimed that the Soviet government created the Yiddish school from the ground up, where none had previously existed.[20]

With the consolidation of Soviet power in the Ukraine and Belorussia (at the end of 1920 and beginning of 1921), the Yiddish-language school began to show both growth and development. In 1920, in that part of Belorussia which remained under Soviet rule, there were sixty-two Yiddish schools. In 1921, when the rest of Belorussia was already under Soviet rule, thirty-eight Yiddish schools were added. These schools had 10,231 children that made up 22½ percent of all Yiddish-speaking children of school age.[21] In the Ukraine, after the civil war and with the consolidation of Soviet power, there were, by the end of 1922, 128 Yiddish schools with 14,983 pupils. This constituted about 1 percent of all the schools in the Ukraine, although Jews were between 6 and 7 percent of the total population.[22] In the following years the Yiddish school showed a substantial growth.

According to the census of 1926, 89.75 percent of the Jews in Belorussia gave Yiddish as their native language. In the few large cities the percentage of Yiddish-speaking Jews was 82.09; in smaller towns the percentage was 94.34; while in the rural districts the percentage was approximately 97. It was natural, therefore, that most of the Yiddish schools were in the small towns. (The decline of the school coincided with the decline of the *shtetl*, which will be discussed later.) A special school census taken in Belorussia in 1927, showed that there were 213 Yiddish schools. In 202 schools the language of instruction was only Yiddish; in seven schools it was Yiddish and Russian; and in four schools, it was Yiddish and Belorussian.

The schools were divided in the following way: 146 four-year schools, 53 seven-year schools, and 2 nine-year schools. Of the Yiddish Russian schools there was 1 four-year and 5 seven-year schools. Of the Yiddish Belorussian schools there was 1 four-year school and 3 seven-year schools. Thus it is evident that 69.5 percent of the Yiddish schools were four-year schools, 28.5 percent seven-year schools, and 1 percent nine-year schools. The schools were divided as follows:

The four-year schools:

In the large cities	22.3%
In the *shtetlech*	53.9%
In the rural districts	1.2%

The seven-year schools:

In the cities	28.7%
In the *shtetlech*	17.3%
In the rural districts	1.5%

The four-year schools were mostly in the small towns (*shtetlech*), and the seven-year schools were in the larger cities. In all the Yiddish schools in Belorussia, 27,124 pupils were enrolled, constituting 46.1 percent of the total number of Jewish children of school age. In these schools, 1,356 teachers were employed.

The same census of 1926 pointed out that in a Jewish school the cost per child was higher than in a Belorussian school, because the Yiddish schools had classes of only about thirty pupils, compared to the Belorussian classes of forty pupils.[23] In 1926, there were 1,532,827 Jews in the Ukraine; 838,732 Jews who lived in the towns gave Yiddish as their native language.[24] According to the breakdown of these figures, in most of the *shtetlech* 90 percent of the Jews spoke Yiddish, but in the larger industrial cities, the percentage dropped down to about 60–58.[25]

The growth of the Yiddish school in the Ukraine is shown by the following figures:

1925	249 schools	number of pupils: 39,474
1926	295 schools	number of pupils: 46,309
1927	393 schools	number of pupils: 61,352
1928	475 schools	number of pupils: 68,836[26]

In the following years, the Yiddish schools expanded. The figures that are given are often conflicting. One source gives the following:

1930   786 schools with 82,414 pupils
1931   831 schools with 94,872 pupils[27]

Another source states that there were 785 schools with 82,000 pupils at the end of 1930.[28] This figure shows that about 50 percent of all the Jewish children of school age attended Yiddish schools. By the beginning of 1931, there were 1,100 Yiddish schools in the Soviet Union with an enrollment of 130,000.[29] Another source gives the following figures for the years 1933–34 in the Ukraine: four- and seven-year Yiddish schools totaled 467; pupils numbered 85,489.[30]

In Great Russia, or the Russian Soviet Socialist Republic, with its great cities, the capital, Moscow, and Leningrad, there were few Yiddish schools. The Jews preferred to send their children to the Russian-language schools. The Jewish Communists could not compel the children to attend Yiddish schools, and there were no outside pressures as there were in Belorussia or the Ukraine. However, there were Yiddish schools in the Crimea, which was at that time part of the Russian Republic (now it is part of the Ukraine), and in the Jewish autonomous region of Birobidzhan, which was also part of the Russian Republic. In both regions about 6,000 Jewish children attended the Yiddish-language schools.[31]

It must be pointed out that compulsory education was not fully initiated until 1930, and that part of the school budget was covered by tuition fees that children of the former bourgeoisie had to pay. Children whose parents were workers, belonging to the trade unions, did not have to pay tuition.[32]

While the early dream of building a Yiddish university had not been realized, a number of teacher-training institutes, known as pedagogical *tekhnikums,* were established. There were also tekhnikums that specialized in training engineers, industrial technicians, medical technicians, and agricultural engineers (agronomists). There was a Yiddish department at the Western Communist University in Moscow that trained qualified functionaries for the Jewish national regions, for the local Jewish towns and regional Soviets, and special cadres of journalists for both the central and local Yiddish press. At the Moscow Yiddish State Theater, there was a

training school for Yiddish actors, under the direction of Solomon
Mikhoels (1890–1948),[33] the leading actor and director of the
Yiddish theater of Moscow. There were also machine-building
tekhnikums where the students learned how to build a variety of
machines. Altogether there were eight pedagogical tekhnikums,
among them one medical and one theatrical, and fifteen industrial
and agricultural. The accomplishments of the pedagogical schools
can be illustrated from the example of the achievement of the
pedagogical tekhnikum of Smolensk; in the period from 1921 to
1935, it graduated five hundred students who became teachers in
the various Yiddish schools in the Soviet Union.

In the machine-construction tekhnikum at Kharkov, in 1935,
there were 500 students who learned how to build machines at the
school. All the machines produced there bore the inscription, both
in Yiddish and Russian, "The Kharkov Jewish Machine Construction Tekhnikum." By 1935, 200 graduates were employed at
the various machine-construction plants in Kharkov, Lugansk,
Magnitogorsk, and Kolumno. The Yiddish agronomical tekhnikums produced specialists who worked both in the Jewish and
non-Jewish collective farms.[34]

By the mid-thirties, the Yiddish school system in the Soviet Union
reached its zenith. There were elementary, secondary, and industrial schools, teacher-training schools, and a Yiddish department at
the Moscow Western University. Between 1935 and 1936, a decline started, due to the following causes:

a. The liquidation of the Jewish sections of the Communist
Party;

b. The concentration of the Jewish people in the large
industrial centers;

c. The great purges and the end of the Belorussianization
in Belorussia and Ukrainization in the Ukraine.

NOTES

1. Grigori Evseyevich Zinoviev (original name Radomislowski) (1883–1936)
   joined the Bolshevik Party in 1903; close collaborator of Lenin. Chairman of
   the III (Communist) International. Executed in 1936 for alleged plotting
   against the regime. Leo Kamenev (originally Lev Borisovich Rosenfeld)
   (1883–1936) joined the Bolshevik party. From 1918 to 1926 was chairman of
   the Moscow Soviet, and from 1922 to 1926 was member of the Political Bureau of the Communist Party; was executed in August 1936 for alleged plotting against Stalin and the Soviet government. Maxim Litvinov (originally

Meier Wallach) (1876–1951): 1918–1930 was Deputy Foreign Minister and in 1930 became Foreign Minister and represented the Soviet Union at the League of Nations 1934–1938; Soviet Ambassador in the U.S. 1941–1943; died in Moscow in 1951.

2. The entire report was republished in the *Tsaitshrift*, Vol. 4, Minsk, 1930.

3. S. Agurski, *Der Yidisher Arbeter in der Komunistisher Bavegung*, Minsk, 1925, pp. iii–v.

4. A. Tchemerinski, *Di Alfarbandishe Komunistishe Partei Bolshevikes un di Yidishe Masn*, Moscow, 1926, pp. 30 ff.

5. See note 31, Chapter VI.

6. About the Jewish Commissariat, see Agurski, *op. cit.*, pp. 6 ff.

7. *A Yor Arbet fun der Russlender Komunistisher Partei in der Yidisher Svive* (A Year's Work of the Russian Communist Party in the Jewish Environment), Moscow, 1924, pp. 6 ff.

8. *Ibid.*, p. 8.

9. *Ibid.*, p. 20.

10. *Ibid.*, p. 33.

11. *Ibid.*, p. 36.

12. Esther (Maria) Frumkin, "Vegn di Nontste Oyfgabn un dem Inhalt fun der Arbet fun di Yidsektsies" (About the Immediate Problems and the Content of the Work of the Jewish Sections), in *A Yor Arbet, op. cit.*, pp. 40 ff.

13. M. Levitan, "Vegn Kultur Arbet," *A Yor Arbet, op. cit.*, pp. 44 ff.

14. *Ibid.*, pp. 48 ff.

15. *Ibid.*, p. 63.

16. *Rezolutsies* (Resolutions), adopted by the All-Ukrainian Conference of Jewish Sections of the Communist Party, 15–20th October, 1925, published Kiev, 1926.

17. *Ibid.*, pp. 14 ff.

18. *Ibid.*, pp. 57, 58.

19. I. Dardak, "Unzere Dergreikhungen far 15 Yor Oktiaber ofn Gebit fun Folk Bildung" (Our Achievements for 15 Years of October [Revolution] in the Field of Public Education), in *Almanak Tsum XV Yorteg fun der Oktiaber Revolutsie, Sotsial-Ekonomisher Zamlbuch*, Minsk, 1932, p. 147.

20. *Ibid.*, pp. 146 ff.

21. *Ibid.*, p. 152.

22. *Statistika Ukrainy* Series VII, Education, Vol. III, Issue I, pp. 9 ff.

23. Y. Paikin, "Einike Sakhaklen fun der Demografisher Tseilung fun 1926" (Some Balances of the Census of 1926), in *Tsaitshrift*, Vaisrusise Visnshaft Akademie, Yidisher Sektor, Vol. 4, Minsk, 1930, pp. 178 ff.

24. Y. Kantor, *Di Yidishe Bafelkerung in Ukraine* (The Jewish Population in the Ukraine), according to Census of 1926, Government Publishing House of the Ukraine, Kiev, 1929, p. 27.

25. *Ibid.*, p. 31.

26. Y. Kantor, *Natsionalnoe Stroitelstvo Sredi Yevreev SSSR* (National Construction Among Jews in the U.S.S.R.), Moscow, 1934, pp. 172 ff.

27. *Ibid.*

28. S. Klitenik, *Kultur Arbet Tsvishn di Yidishe Arbetndike inem Ratn Farband*

(Cultural Work Among the Jewish Toilers in the Soviet Union), Moscow, 1931, pp. 9, 10.

29. *Ibid.*, p. 10.

30. "Kultur Boyung Tsvishn di Yidishe Masn" (Cultural Construction Among the Jewish Masses), in *Yidn in F.S.S.R.* (Jews in the U.S.S.R.), Moscow, 1935, p. 262.

31. Klitenik, *op. cit.*, pp. 10 ff.

32. Dardak, *op. cit.*, p. 153; Paikin, *op. cit.*, p. 189.

33. Mikhoels' original name was Solomon Vovsi. He was killed by the Secret Police upon Stalin's order on January 13, 1948.

34. *Yidn in F.S.S.R.*, *op. cit.*, pp. 264–266; Klitenik, *op. cit.*, p. 12.

CHAPTER 8

The Curriculum and the
Jewish Content of the
Yiddish-Language School

ONE writer defined the Jewish school in the Soviet Union as, "simply a Soviet school with Yiddish as the language of instruction; no deviations from the standard curriculum are tolerated."[1] It is true that the Yiddish school was a Soviet school, its curriculum strictly regulated by the government. However, it differed from the non-Jewish school not only by using Yiddish as the language of instruction, but by teaching Yiddish and Yiddish literature as separate subjects. In the pedagogical schools, Jewish history was taught, though of course from a Marxist and Communist point of view. Although Jewishness was not stressed, these schools gave a pupil the knowledge that he was different from his Ukrainian and Belorussian neighbors, that he was a Jew.

Instruction in Yiddish had a nationalizing effect on the pupils. Absence of religious instruction and elimination of all national aspects of Jewish life left the Yiddish language as the only factor to remind the children that they were Jewish. However, the Yiddish language is full of national Jewish values, of specific idiomatic expressions, and it is saturated with Jewish folk sayings. Although this view of the influence of the Jewish language upon the children has been challenged, in response, two points may be made. Most

97

of the Jewish Communists who joined the Party in 1919 came from the Jewish Labor Bund, from the Poale Zion, and from the Socialist Territorialists. Many had received a Jewish religious education and had been brought up in a strict Jewish atmosphere. Some of them came from the yeshivot where they had prepared for the rabbinate; but a religious education did not prevent them from becoming Communists and carrying out the revolution on the "Jewish Street," nor did it always assure the retention of Jewish values. However, attendance at the Yiddish school did create a certain consciousness of being a Jew, of being different from non-Jewish neighbors.[2]

Secondly, Yiddish literature was taught at all levels of the Yiddish school, and included the works of Mendele Mokher Seforim, Sholem Aleichem, and Peretz in addition to the later writers and Soviet Yiddish writers. Though the works studied were selected and were taught from a Communist point of view, the children, nonetheless, studied classical, pre-classical and post-classical Yiddish literature. The nationalizing effect on the children surely cannot be doubted. Therefore, the introductory statement that the "Jewish school is simply a Soviet school with Yiddish as the language of instruction" is both true and not entirely true.

The Yiddish-language Soviet school went through the same stages and regulations as all other schools. There were times when no homework was assigned, when the children spent many hours on walks and excursions, and when discipline was loose. When discipline was restored, when the spirit of competition and challenge was reintroduced, the same was applied in the Yiddish-language school. With the consolidation of Stalin's power at the end of the twenties, the school was reformed and rebuilt, to conform to the industrialization of the country and to the expansion of the sciences.

In 1930, the Central Committee of the Communist Party of the Soviet Union issued a document which gave directives to all the schools in the Soviet Union. The Yiddish-language schools adopted all its regulations. According to this document,

> The Soviet school, which aims to prepare fully developed members for the communist society, gives the children a wider social and political horizon and general development than the former pre-revolutionary bourgeois school. In the last years, the quality of education has improved in the Soviet school. Great success has been

achieved after the historical decision of the 16th Party Congress to introduce obligatory schooling. . . . But in spite of all achievements, the Central Committee states that the Soviet school does not meet the colossal demands of socialist construction. The Central Committee maintains that the drawback of our school at the present time is a curriculum which does not include enough general education and does not solve, in a satisfactory way, the problem of preparing enough graduates, thoroughly acquainted with the fundamentals of physics, chemistry, mathematics, native tongue and geography, for the tekhnikums and colleges. Therefore, our schools do not develop our children as fully qualified builders of socialism, who combine theory with practice.

The document further stated that the Soviet school aimed to produce trained workers who should be good Communists, well educated politically; and that the pupils should be acquainted with the practical needs of building socialism, the application of electricity, chemistry, physics, mathematics, and agronomy. It was felt that this type of education could be insured by a school that stressed both political and technical education. Education was declared obligatory for all children from the age of eight to seventeen, effective July 25, 1930. The elementary and secondary schools were unified into a ten-year school, though separate elementary and secondary schools remained in operation. However, the graduates of the elementary school were admitted automatically into the secondary school.

The same document continued:

> To instruct the departments of education of the various republics, to organize immediately the scientific Marxist revision of the school curricula and to insure in the curriculum clearly marked systematized courses in the native language, mathematics, physics, chemistry, geography, and history, the introduction of this program must take place not later than January 1, 1932. Simultaneous with the revision of the curriculums, the departments of education must adopt means to put the revised curriculum into effect.
>
> In the Soviet school, applying the various new methods of teaching that can help to educate and prepare active participants in socialist construction makes it necessary to start a decisive struggle against the easygoing project method. A struggle must be conducted against the system of the project method. The attempts which adhered to the anti-Leninist theory of the dying of the school, and made the project method the foundation of our curriculum, led to

the deterioration of our school. The Central Committee decrees that the departments of education of the Union Republics organize immediately and place scientific research work on a higher plane, mobilize the best party functionaries to this work, and rebuild the curriculum on a solid Marxist-Leninist foundation.

The foundation of communist education is polytechnical education, which gives the pupils the fundamentals of science, acquaints them, both in theory and practice, with all the main branches of the industry, and creates a close contact of education with production work—the departments of education of the Union Republics are therefore ordered during 1931, to expand the workshops in the schools and see that the expansion of the workrooms is accompanied by a closer tie with the factories and collective farms. The fusion of the general curriculum with production work should be accomplished in a way to make the production work of the pupils a main object of education. The factories and the collective farms must help the departments of education attain this aim by supplying the schools with workbenches and laboratories; by assigning to the schools skilled workers and specialists, who would participate directly in the work of the school; and by helping the pedagogues to acquire the skill of teaching production work.

The departments of education of the Union Republics must organize model schools in each region and in all cities, and place these schools in a financially better situation. These schools must have the best pedagogical cadres, in order that the teachers, workers, collective farmers, and pupils should learn from this special school how to build the polytechnic school.

In order to facilitate the political technicalization of the school, during 1931–32, the department of education of the Union Republics should organize a number of polytechnical museums and special polytechnical sections at the various museums. The Supreme Council for people's economy should help in this work both financially and in organizing these museums. The department of education, with the government publishing houses, must establish libraries for the pupils and the teachers in their native languages. The department of education, with the movie organizations, must develop a plan to utilize the movies for the school and for its polytechnicalization.

In the period of socialism, when the proletariat carries through the complete destruction of the class society, Communist education is a thing of extreme importance.

In this connection, the Central Committee directs the party organizations to strengthen the Communist ideology of the school and to supervise the introduction of the socio-political curriculum in the seven-year school and in the pedagogical tekhnikums.

In accordance with the urgency of the decrees of the Central Committee of July 25, 1930, concerning universal obligatory elementary education, the Central Committee of the All-Union Council of People's Commissars, proposes that this decree be immediately put in force and that all children up to the age of seventeen, receive a polytechnical education.[3]

From these decrees, it is obvious that the new curriculum applied to all schools in the Soviet Union, including the Yiddish schools. The decree also stipulated that the teaching of the native language should be strengthened, which helped the position of the Yiddish-language school, and the teaching of Yiddish.

As expected, the various departments of education of the Union Republics began to enforce the new regulations. The administrators, supervisors, and teachers of the Yiddish-language schools followed suit with even more zeal, and within a short time, the Yiddish school was fitted into the Soviet school system.

As was customary in the Soviet Union, the educators not only had to put the new regulations into effect, they had to "confess" their previous mistakes. These "confessions" are evidence of the lot of the Soviet teacher and educator, for they present a picture of the difficulties of education in the Soviet Union at that time. The "confessions" of the Yiddish educators recreate the atmosphere of the Yiddish school and the difficult task of the educators.

We present here a confession, written by the leading Yiddish educator, I. Dardak:

> The decree of the Central Committee about the introduction of universal education, and its implementation by the end of the first Five-Year Plan, was one of the mightiest blows at the Rightist opportunists and national democrats in the field of public education. The two-party conference of the Central Committee of the Communist Party of Belorussia and the all-Union conference about peoples' education, formulated the methods of conversion of the school to a political-technological school, to a school that should fit the demands of socialist construction. In the decree of June 25, 1930, the second conference, the main lines of universal, obligatory education on the basis of a seven-year school are pointed out. The aim is to bring the school closer to the factory and manufacturing process.

The decree helped the school to step forward towards the production process, and to create the conditions for a real polytechnical school.

But here the class enemy does not sleep. Conducting his tactics for a national religious education, the class enemy appears now with a placard of "left" phrases against the polytechnological school.

Left opportunism, as an agent of the petit bourgeoisie in the cities, has formed a theory in the field of education that the school is dying; that the natural influences from the surrounding atmosphere are the most important factors in education; that the curriculum in the school should be built so as to give education what is essential for practical labor.

The whole concept of this theory is based on the wish to revise the party program regarding the development of the fully developed personality. The Leftists have proposed the conversion of the polytechnological school into a technological school only, into a guild of contractors, a school that does not give a sufficient norm of knowledge which is essential for socialist construction. This theory as an expression of the tactics of the class enemy that wants to destroy the polytechnological school, found its strongest expression in the writings of Comrade Rives and in the writings of the author of this article.

Comrade Rives, conducting a struggle against the Right, conducted the struggle not from Marxist-Leninist positions, but from the positions of Menshevik idealism. Already in 1926, Comrade Rives developed the thesis of idealizing the empirical pedagogy of John Dewey, completely built on the principles of Dewey's instrumentalist philosophy, which is based completely on the principle of the American bourgeoisie that Time is Money, and therefore, only that which is needed for utilitarian purposes should be taught. Dewey proposes therefore that theoretical work must be subordinated to practice. This theory is essentially to prepare the worker as a supplement to the machine, a slave of the bourgeoisie—a fascist system. This theory was idealized by Comrade Rives as late as 1926. He wrote: "In order to solve the problem of method in schoolwork, we must get acquainted with the basic method of the biggest American schools, that have the right to be called workschools. It is known that John Dewey is the greatest pedagogue of our time, in whose work we find not only propaganda but instructions how to build the work-school."

In Dewey's works, there are the following principles, without which, according to Rives, the work-school cannot be created. These principles are: (1) Instruction must be thoroughgoing. (2) Theoretical work must be subordinated to practice. (3) The school has to influence the surroundings. The best way to carry out these principles is through the project method.

The same theory found a place in the essays and lectures of the author of this article. The present author developed the Leftist-opportunist theory that the school is dying. He developed the thesis that the whole curriculum should be subordinated to the filling out of the production schedule at the factory. The school has become a guild at the plant, a collective farm. Together with this thesis, he developed the theory that the school should function by only one method, that he called the method of socialist challenge, which was the same project method under a disguise. This meant carrying through the Project Method under the mask of socialist competition. He also developed a theory that the school had to abolish grade systems and adopt the system of rings or steps, which led to the ruining of the school. Such a Leftist-opportunist conception is another example of how the class enemy influences the weakly disciplined elements and they become, objectively, agents of the class enemy that strives to destroy socialist construction.

About my Leftist-opportunist conception and errors, I spoke and wrote a number of times. I also uncovered the class roots of this conception. But, although I recognized my opportunist errors and conceptions, this theory remained in my writings, and they brought a great deal of harm in practice.

Although the school has become polytechnological, there is still one fault with our present school—that the pupils do not yet receive sufficient knowledge, that the schools do not prepare students fully for the engineering schools and colleges.

But the new decrees deliver a deathblow to the Rightist-opportunists who want to drag the school backwards, retain the old scholastic verbal school, restore the old bourgeois school; and it also delivers a deathblow to the Leftist-opportunists who wish to ruin the school, who do not appreciate fully the value of theory, who deny the important part of the teacher, who have a purely empirical approach to the preparation of cadres and are against the polytechnological school, and are in favor of a purely technical school.[4]

Only a short time after the new program was issued, it was adopted by the Yiddish schools as reported in the following document, published in 1931:

> Our Yiddish Soviet work-schools (as well as the schools of the other nationalities) have rebuilt their structure. A number of Yiddish schools have been completely rebuilt. The whole curriculum in the school is organized to teach the pupils to operate machines.

They learn the organization of production in various factories and collective farms. For this purpose, each school has to be connected with an industrial plant, with a collective farm, or Soviet farm. The children of the upper groups work a certain number of hours in a factory, industrial plant, and collective farm, and what they do there, see, and observe becomes integrated with what is being taught in the classroom. The younger children work at the shops in the schools and everything that they do there is taught during school hours.

The children, both the younger and the older, accomplish great things at the factories and collective farms. They propagandize their parents and the workers to increase production and the productivity of labor. They demand that their parents become shock troops among the workers, that they enter the collective farms, and conduct socialist competition. The children collect junk, metal pieces in the various plants, they conduct cultural work among the workers, they give theatrical performances, and they issue wall newspapers. All these things they learn at school, and therefore the toiling people always receive the school children warmly. The workers, in turn, teach the children how to work, how to operate the machines, and acquaint them with the division of labor. Mutual evening parties are organized by the school and industrial plant. The factory provides the school with workshops, and all other aid for production work. This way, the children participate in the great socialist construction that goes on in our land. The children have their part in all our successes.

We already have hundreds of Yiddish schools that have been reconstructed and became truly socialist work-schools.[5]

As was customary in the Soviet Union, every decree by the government was always approved, lauded, and popularized. The functionaries of the Jewish schools, naturally, approved the new decrees about the rebuilding of the school and the establishment of the political-technological school. The Jewish functionaries republished the statement by the chairman of the Executive of the government of the Ukraine, M. A. Skrypniak, which read:

> The decree of the Central Committee has definitely given a final blow to the so-called Marxist theoreticians who built our school practice according to the principles of the Project Method, which practically led to the ruin of our school.

> We have revised our whole school practice in the light of the decree and party orders, and we have completely done away with the Project Method and all its consequences.[6]

The curriculum for the school required that the pupils participate fully in a work program. The work was assigned in the following way:

Children   8–10 years old, 4 hours per week;
Children 11–13 years old, 6 hours per week;
Children 14–16 years old, 8 hours per week.[7]

The following schedule gives the curriculum for the Yiddish schools as it was worked out and approved by the authorities of the People's Commissariat for Education.[8] (See table on page 106.)

This curriculum shows that the Yiddish-language school was a Soviet school, but that Yiddish and Yiddish literature occupied an important part in the curriculum, nine hours per week being devoted to them in the first grade, eight hours per week in the second grade, seven hours in the third grade, four in the fourth, three in the fifth, and four in the sixth.

Jewish history was not taught as a separate subject, but in the history course which began in the fifth grade with two hours per week; the history of the Jews was included as part of general history. In the courses in the history of the Communist Party, the history of the Jewish labor and revolutionary movement was included as part of the general labor movement.[9] In a curriculum outline for the teaching of Yiddish and Yiddish literature, issued for the Yiddish schools by the People's Commissariat of Education, there was an introduction which stated:

> The subject of Yiddish in our school was, until now, in a state of confusion. The Yiddish school developed in a period of revolution, it had neither previous experience nor traditions, and had to start all over at the very beginning. The majority of our teachers came either from a Russian or Hebrew school, and some were untrained teachers who received their education at a Russian school. It is no wonder, then, that the teaching of Yiddish was not on a proper plane. No program stated what to teach and the methods of teaching. There was no unity of program, and no fast-set curriculum. The new program aims to set a standard for systematic teaching of Yiddish and to formulate a program for teaching.
>
> The teaching of Yiddish has to encompass talking, reading, writing, and observation about the development of the language. From the first day, we must strive to develop a clear, connected, compressed, and understandable language. The teacher must demand from the child short but correct answers on single questions, and

HOURS PER WEEK FOR EACH SUBJECT IN GRADES 1–10

Subjects	1st	2nd	3rd	4th	5th	6th	7th	8th	9th	10th
Yiddish and Yiddish Lit.	9	8	7	6	5	4	2	7	6	7
Ukrainian in Ukraine; Belorussian in Belorussia			3	4	3					
Astronomy										1
Russian				3	3	3				
Biology	1	2	2	3	2	2	2	2		
Geology										1
Geography			2	3	2	2	2	2	2	2
Music	1	1	1	1	1	1				
History					2	2	2	5	4	4
Drawing							1	1	1	1
History of Communist Party									3	2
A foreign language; German or French					3	2	2	3	3	3
Chemistry							2	2	2	2
Mathematics	5	5	5	5	5	5	4	4	5	5
Physics						3	3	4	2	3

then proceed to a collective, short, consolidated story. The language should be simple, not artful, at the same time casual. The material for talking and writing should be that which the pupil sees, observes, and what he hears. The talk should be connected with the season, surrounded with the real and practical. The child has to learn not only the poetic language, or the language of writers, but also the exact scientific language, newspaper language, etc. The child has to be trained how to read both serious artistic works and popular-scientific material, as well as newspapers and journals. The intonation of sentence and the sentence must be stressed.

Some attention should be paid to grammar. The time is gone when grammar was looked upon as a means of teaching how to write, read, and talk. Scientific grammar has other aims; scientific grammar introduces into the language, into the sounds of the language, form and meaning. Grammar also explains the evolution and development of language.

Grammar, orthography, morphology are acquired by the children in the process of doing, through the awakened activity and interest of the children. The teacher does not present ready-made knowledge, but he strives to get from the pupils an independent formulation, of a grammatical rule or law.[10]

The program outline then states what to teach in the various grades. The literary material was to be grouped around various themes, such as village, *shtetl,* city, labor and the revolutionary movement, World War and Revolution.

Grade I or Group I: reading easy stories;

Grade II or Group II: reading stories, making up an ending for a story;

Grade or Group III: reading literary and popular scientific works, writing a composition about episodes and events that the pupil observed or lived through;

Group IV: reading individually, either long stories or fragments of novels, to analyze on basis of material read the social life of the hero, occupation. Giving a short characterization of characters in novel. Marking down all new words encountered;

Group V: poetry, prose, the peculiarities of the poetic language, rhythm, basic knowledge about sentence construction, analysis of form of a work. Discussion about poems read and analysis;

Group VI: reading individually classical works; analysis of poetic form, rhymes, metaphors, personification, epic and lyric poetry, dramatic works. Analysis of dialects of the Yiddish language, analysis of form, word order;

Group VII: reading of complicated classical works, history of language, history of Yiddish. The death of languages—Hebrew. The influences of one language on another. Classification of language.

Recitation, dramatization, preparation of oral talks about literature, and learning how to participate in a literary discussion.[11]

The literature to be used according to Themes:

The Village

Abramovitch, Shalom Yaacov (Mendele Mokher Seforim): *Shlome Reb Khaims, Fishke der Krumer* (Fishke the Cripple)

Sholem Aleichem (Shalom Rabinovich): *Tevye der Milkhiger* (Tevye the Milkman)

Kassel, David: *In Dorf* (In the Village)

Bergelson, David: *Nokh Alemen* (After All)

Opatoshu, Joseph: *In Poilishe Velder* (In Polish Woods), *Alein* (Alone)

Ignatov, David: *Fibi*

Raboy, Isaac: *A Pas Yam* (Horizon on Sea)

Turgeniev: *Mumu*

Saltykov-Shchedrin, N.: *How One Peasant Brought Up Two Generals*

Grigorovitch: *The Peasant*

Korolenko: *Little Dogs*

Serafimovitch: *A Village Meeting*

Seifulina: *Earth*

Ivanov: *Partisans*

Hugo, Victor: *The Year 93*

Kotik, Yehezkiel: *Memoirs*

Hofshtein, David: *In Dorf, Vinter Farnakht* (In the Village, In Winter at Dusk)

Einhorn, David: *Di Sazhlke* (The Stream)

Giavanelli: *Spartac*

Stowe, Harriet Beecher: *Uncle Tom's Cabin*

The Town (Shtetl)

Abramovitch: *Vintch-Fingerl* (Magic Ring), *Shlome Reb Khaims,
Fishke der Krumer* (Fishke the Cripple)
Sholem Aleichem: *Kasrilevke*
Peretz, Y. L.: *Reyzebilder* (Travel Pictures)
Asch, Sholem: *A Shtetl, In Koyler Gesl* (A Town, in Koyler
Street)
Reisen, Abraham: *Di Kleit, Di Fabrik* (The Store, The Factory)
Weissenberg: *A Shtetl* (A Town)
Markish, Peretz: *Volhynia*
Einhorn: *Litvishe Motivn* (Lithuanian Motifs)
Kulbak, Moishe: *Lithuania*
Rolnik, I.: *Lithuania*

The City

Hofshtein, David: *The City*
Naidus, Leib: *From the City*
Halpern, Moshe Leib: *The City*
Mani Leib: *The City*
Abramovitch: *At Leizer the Tailor's*
Reisen, Abraham: *The Dog*
Rosenfeld, Yona: *The Thief*
Chekhov: *Vanka*
Andreyev, Leonid: *Peter at a Summer Place*
London, Jack: *Strike*
Seifulina: *Criminals*
Neverov: *Tashkent, City of Bread*
Gorki: *My Childhood*
Weissenberg, I. M.: *Dor Halekh ve Dor Bo* (A Generation
Passes)
Peretz, Y. L.: *Four Generations; The Meshulakh; Who Is More
Beautiful? The Stranger's Wedding Dress*
Sholem Aleichem: *Menachem Mendl; Mentchn* (People)
An-Ski, S. I.: *The Struggle for Life*
Libin, Z.: *Ten Years; Dream of Padalkin*
Yushkevitch, Simon: *Hunger*
Ignatov, David: *In the Caldron*
Zola, Emile: *Germinal*
Sinclair, Upton: *King Coal*

London, Jack: *Iron Heel*
Abramovitch: *The Tax, The Draft*
Kharik, I.: *Muds of Minsk*
Gildin, Hayim: *In the Factory, My Hammer*
Broderzon, M.: *Dawn*
Folk Songs from Ginzburg: Marek Collection
Idioms from Collection of A. Bernstein and Prilutzki
An-ski: *In the Stream; Foter un Zun* (Father and Son)
Kobrin, Leon: *Barukh*
Kassel, David: *Meier from the Little Bund*
Olgin, M. J.: *Ven Keytn Klingen* (When Chains Ring)
Asch, Sholem: *Mary* (not to be confused with the later novel of
    the same name)
Stepniak: *A House Near the Volga*
Mirabeau, J.: *John and Madelaine*
Gorki, Maxim: *The Mother*
Lidsin, Yurk: *From the Distant North*
Leivick, H.: *Siberian Poems*

World War and Revolution
Barbusse, Henri: *Le Feu* (The Fire)
Kellerman: *Ninth of November*
John Reed: *Ten Days That Shook the World*
Godiner: *Rings, Ivangorod*
Lebedinski: *The Week*
Epelbaum, A.: *"Oyf-Broyz"*
Warshavsky, Oyzer: *Smugglers*
Hofshtein: *Procession, October*
Kushnirov, Aron: *Russia*
Gildin, Hayim: *Triumph*
Broderzon, M.: *The March*
Babel, Isaac: *Stories*[12]

The program also presented a poem to analyze, and discussed
methods of analysis.

In Shtetl
fun David Hofshtein
Dort iber shtet hot shoyn geklungen
Fun shpitz fun turem i eins, i tsvey
In thom fun nakht, in land fun shney
Is eins a derfel farzunken.

Vi inzelekh fun mentshn ru
In shtroy farbilt, af nakht farvarimt
Mit shotn afn pleyt in shlof gearemt
Far haizele a haizl halt zikh tsu.

Di shterndike shtilkayt halt zich ein
In shtiln otem fun lobn
In heizl einem iz farblibn
A shtile rod fun lompn shayn.

Di shlofedike vinklekh hern koym
Fun tish a shorkh fun bleter
Nor yunge oygn vern alts nit zeter.

In the Village
by David Hofshtein

There, over the cities, has already rung out
From the steeple's spire, one . . . two . . .
In the abyss of night, in the land of snow
A tiny village lies buried.

Like islets of human rest
Wrapped in straw, warm against the night
With shadows on the fence embraced in sleep
One little house clings to the other.

The starry silence is prolonged
In the quiet breath of life.
In one tiny house there still remains
A quiet circle of lamplight.

The sleeping corners scarcely hear
A rustle of pages on the table:
Only young eyes are never sated.

Analysis

What kind of image is evoked in the poem? Tell it in your own words.

How many pictures does the poem create? Can the poem be divided into the following divisions?—Time, village, house.

How does the poet describe time?

The poet tells us that the clock strikes two—but can you find the time without the clock's striking two?

What meaning and significance have the words "i eins, i tsvey" ("both"—both one and two)?
Does the poet mark the intermission between one and two?
Can the word "I" be substituted by "Un" (and) or not?
"In thom fun nakht—what image or picture did the poet evoke with this sentence?
Has the word "thom" a real meaning or is it a metaphor?
"In land fun shney"—in the land of snow—what meaning has this expression? Is it a limited view or a broad one? Has the poet made the picture darker by using the word *thom?*
"Vi inzelech fun mentchn ru" (like little islands of human rest)— Is the comparison logical, exact? Can one compare the appearance of the village with a little island? What is the meaning of "mentchn ru"? How do the houses appear in the village? Has the village the attributes of a living person? Is the village personified?
Is there an emotional element in the sentence "In shlof gearemt"? Do the words "haizele," "inzele" have an emotional meaning? How many times is the sound "sh" repeated (in "shtiln otem, a shtile rod")?
How many beats has the first line?
What is the difference between the words "shlofedike" and "shleferike"?
Read the third stanza and state what words are accented.
Is the tone of the poem a quiet one?
Does the serenity and petrified state of the surroundings express the exciting mood and restlessness of the poet?
Does the poem give a picture of the average village in Russia?[13]

A slightly revised program for the teaching of Yiddish and Yiddish literature was issued in 1927, by the Central Jewish Education Bureau of the People's Commissariat for Education in Belorussia.

> Grade I: Teaching to read simple stories, children should be trained to tell, in their own language, what they see. Correct answers to simple questions. Learning, by heart, simple poems. Instruction about period at end of a sentence, question mark, and exclamation mark. Learn the words: Yid, Yidish, Yingl, Yidene.

> Grade II: Composition, change the person in a story, make up a different ending for a story read, keep a diary and observation of

weather, temperature, read simple stories. Grammar and spelling. Conjugations, prepositions, singular and plural, diminutives.

Grade III: Children to be trained to read artistic and popular-scientific material. Comparison of similar situations in various stories. To enumerate characters in a story, to analyze description of nature. To train the pupil to read a story individually. Reading of extracts from daily newspapers. To write compositions about episodes and events observed, to describe walks, excursions. Children trained to prepare notebooks with clippings of news items, poems, idiomatic expressions, riddles, preparation of minutes about a meeting. Conjugations, prepositions, words to be stressed.

Grade IV: Pupils are trained to read short stories, or fragments of novels. Stressing of family life, home, occupation, time and place, characterization of heroes in the story or novel, evaluation of material read, reading of newspapers, diary of planned work, wall newspaper, composing of news items, minutes of meetings. Grammar.

Grade V: Material to be used:
Hofshtein, D.: poem, *Village*
Opatoshu, J.: *In Polish Woods*
Turgeniev: *Biruk*
Saltykov-Shchedrin: *How One Peasant Brought Up Two Generals*
Raboy, Isaac: *The Jewish Farmer*
Ignatov, David: *Fibi*
Mendele Mokher Seforim: *Fishke der Krumer (Fishke the Cripple), Shlome Reb Khaim's*
Sholem Aleichem: *Mottel the Cantor's Son, From the Fair*, Selections from *Tevye the Milkman, Lekh Lekho*
Kharik, I.: *Bread*
Peretz, Y. L.: *The Meshulakh, Two Brothers*
Asch, Sholem: *Men and Gods*
Markish, Peretz: *Volhynia*
Vinchevsky, Morris: *In the Streets to the Masses*
Shwartzman, Osher: *Insurrection*
Broderzon, Moshe: *Courage*
Suffixes, prefixes, technical terms of tools, poetics, poetry and prose, rhythm, rhyme, metaphors, synonyms.

Grade VI:
Abramovitch, S. Y. (Mendele Mokher Seforim)—*Tevye the Milkman*
Sholem Aleichem: *Selected Letters of Menachem Mendel*
Peretz, Y. L.: *The Fast, Bontche the Silent (Bontche Shveyg)*

Weissenberg: *A Shtetl*
Asch, Sholem: Selections from *"Uncle Moses"* and *"In America"*
    from book *America*
Kharik: *Mud of Minsk*
Hofshtein: *A City*
Leivick, H.: *Siberian Poems*
Gildin, Hayim: *In the Future*
Gorki, M.: *My Childhood*
Gostev: *Stranger Than Words*
Longfellow: *Hiawatha*
Gorki, M.: *Tunnel*
Kushnirov: *Russia*

Analysis of various dialects, syntax, training of the use of handbooks, dictionaries and encyclopedias. The study of drama construction: development of scenes and acts, solution, the characters and their relations to one another.

Grade VII:

A. The idea of folklore, folk songs, idioms, proverbs. A short survey of the literature of the Haskalah, I. M. Levinson, Solomon Ettinger, Aksenfeld, the Haskalah Movement and the Peasant Movement.

Linetsky, Joel: *The Polish Boy*
Mendele Mokher Seforim: *Fishke the Cripple, The Journey of Benjamin III, Shloime Reb Khayim's*
Gordon, Michael: *Poems*

B. The development of capitalism and the rise of Jewish political parties.

Sholem Aleichem: *Old and New, Kasrilevke, Selected Letters of Menachem Mendel*
Peretz, Y. L.: *Travel Pictures, What Does a Jewess Need? Insured, The Rebetzen of Skulek, Three Gifts, Between Two Mountains*
Poems by Simon Frug, Morris Rosenfeld, Morris Vinchevsky, and Abraham Reisen.

C. Materials about the development of the Jewish labor movement and the First Russian Revolution (1905).

Asch: *The Daughter*
Weissenberg: *A Shtetl*
An-ski: *In the Stream, Between Two Revolutions 1906–1917*
Einhorn, David: poems
Bergelson, David: Selections from *After All*
Leivick, H.: *Snow* (from *Siberian Poems*)
Selections of Soviet Yiddish poetry.[14]

This program of teaching literature and the Yiddish language was built mainly around the Project System, which was subsequently eliminated. However, though the Project Method was abolished, the teaching of the language and literature remained essentially the same, and the new textbooks included nearly the same materials, with the exception of Asch, Einhorn, and other "bourgeois" writers. In later editions of the textbooks, the selections of Izy Kharik and Hayim Gildin were discarded, because they had been arrested as enemies of the people. The teaching of Yiddish and Yiddish literature was adjusted to fit the number of hours allotted to it, according to the schedule.

The curriculum at the Jewish Pedagogical Tekhnikums or Teachers' Seminaries, at the Jewish departments of the Western University at Moscow, and at the Jewish departments of the Universities of Odessa, Minsk, Kharkov, included full courses in Yiddish literature and Jewish history, as well as general pedagogical studies. The Teachers' Institutes and the Jewish departments of the various universities prepared teachers for the Yiddish schools; the university departments also provided functionaries for the Jewish city soviets, for the Jewish courts, and for the Jewish collective farms.

Presented here is a curriculum of a Jewish Pedagogical Tekhnikum as well as of the Jewish Department of the Pedagogical Faculty of the University of Minsk:

Course I

Jewish Social Movements
Seminar for Jewish Social Movements
Seminar for Yiddish Literature
Seminar for Political Economy
Yiddish Language
Textbooks:
Zalman Reizen: *Yiddish Grammar*
Kalmanovitch: *Syllabus for Lectures about Yiddish Grammar*
Zabrov: *Literary Chrestomathy*
Extracts from classical literature

Course II

History of the Jews in Lithuania
Ukraine and Belorussia
Seminar for Yiddish Literature
Yiddish Folklore

Literature: Ginzburg and Marek—*Folk Songs*
J. L. Cahan: *Yiddish Folk Songs*
Bernstein: *Yiddish Proverbs*
Ravnitzky: *Jewish Jokes*
Lehman: *Work and Freedom*
Yiddish Language: 4 hours per week
Hebrew Language: 2 hours per week

Course III

Pedagogy: 4 hours
Methods of Teaching Language and Literature: 2 hours
Old Hebrew Literature: 4 hours
Literature or texts to be used:
   Eliashev, P. (Baal Makhshoves): *Writings*
   Litvakov, M.: *In Umru*, Part I
   Reizen, Zalman: *Lexicon of Yiddish Literature*
   Oyslender, Nahum: *Main Trends of Yiddish Realism*
   Niger, S.: *About Yiddish Writers*
   Pines: *History of Yiddish Literature*
Introduction to Germanics: 4 hours

Course IV

Grammar of Early Yiddish
References:
   Veynger: *Syllabus of Lectures*
   Landau and Vachshtein: *Private Yiddish Letters of 1619*
   Kaufman: *Memoirs of Glickel Hamel*
   Weinreich, Max: *Megilat Vintz*
First One Hundred Years of Research in History of Yiddish
Grammar
Grammar of Yiddish
References:
   Veynger: *Lectures About Yiddish*
   Prilutzki, Noah: *Dialectological Notes*
Contemporary Yiddish Literature: 4 hours
References:
   Litvakov, M.: *In Umru*, Part II
   Oyslender, Nahum: *Veg Ein, Veg Oys*
   Reizen, Zalman: *Lexicon of Yiddish Literature*
   Eliashev (Baal Makhshoves): *Writings*
Yiddish Folklore: 4 hours
School Practice: 4 hours
Seminar, Yiddish Literature
History of Jewish Art: 2 hours
Yiddish Language: 2 hours

Socio-Political Department
Course II
Yiddish: 4 hours
History of Jews in Lithuania, Ukraine, and Belorussia
Seminar in History
Seminar in Economics

Course III
Pedagogy: 4 hours
Methods of Studying Sociology: 2 hours
History of the Jews in Russia in the nineteenth and the twentieth
  centuries: 2 hours
History of Yiddish Literature: 2 hours
Yiddish Language: 2 hours

Course IV
History of Russia in period of finance capital and the imperialist
  war: 3 hours
History of Jewish Public Education: 2 hours
History of New Yiddish Literature
School Practice: 4 hours
Seminar: Historical Materialism: 2 hours
Yiddish: 2 hours

Physics-Mathematics Section
Course I
Yiddish Language: 4 hours
Jewish Social Movements: 4 hours

Course II
Methodics of Mathematics: 4 hours
Methodics of Physics: 2 hours
Pedagogy: 4 hours
School Practice: 4 hours
III and IV courses, physics and mathematics, pedagogy, school
  practice and Yiddish[15]

This curriculum remained in force until about 1928. It was
then attacked as a bourgeois, Zionist, Nationalist-Democratic-
Yiddishistic-Menshevik curriculum, and was revised. Hebrew and
Semitic philology were removed from the curriculum, and hours
were added to the teaching of Russian history, Marxism, and dialec-
tical materialism. Even with the revisions the curriculum retained
a great deal of Jewish content, especially Yiddish and Yiddish lit-

erature. Works by foreign Yiddish scholars, Kalmanovitch, Wein-reich, Zalman Reizen and N. Prilutski were removed from the reference books, as well as the critical works of S. Niger and Baal Machshoves. Works by Soviet Yiddish critics, folklorists, and scholars were substituted.[16]

The Jewish Section of the Second Western Moscow University was reorganized in March 1926. It had been founded in 1922 as the Yiddish linguistic section for the study of Yiddish and Yiddish literature. Its aim was to prepare teachers for the advanced classes of the Yiddish-language schools, with this curriculum:

I Year

	hours per week
Foundation of industrialization and agriculture	4
Introduction to education	2
Foundations of Pedagogy	4
Economics	2
Historical materialism	2
German, French, or English	2
Technical work	3
Military training	2
Physical culture	2
Yiddish	4
Hebrew	2
Yiddish literature reading	4
History of the Jews in modern times	2
General philology	3
	38

II Year

	hours per week
Agricultural reconstruction and the 5-year plan	2
Pedagogy	6
Pedology	4
Shopwork	3
Physical culture	2
Dialectical materialism, Leninism	2

Russian literature in the nineteenth century	2
West-European literature, to the nineteenth century	2
History of finance capitalism	2
German	2
Yiddish literary language	3
New Yiddish literature	3
Early history of Jews of Middle Ages	2
Economics	2
Hebrew	2
Military training	2
	39

III Year

hours per week

Pedagogy	4
Pedagogy and pedology	2
National policy and Socialist construction among the Jews	2
History of industrial and finance capitalism in the West and in Russia	4
Military training	2
History of the Communist Party and of the Jewish labor movement	2
Yiddish literature in the twentieth century	4
Folklore and early Yiddish literature	2
Methodology of literature and language	4
Russian and West-European literature in the twentieth century	4
History of Yiddish	2
Methodology of literature	2
Ukrainian or Belorussian	1
	35

IV Year

hours per week

Pedagogy	2
Leninism	2
Military training	1

Politics	2
Yiddish grammar	2
Methodology of Yiddish language, literature, and school practice	8
Yiddish dialects	2
Special seminar of Yiddish literature	2
Methodology of social sciences	2
	23[17]

The school (Jewish Section of the Second Western Moscow University) started with twelve students, and in 1929 it had one hundred.

M. Shpierayn prepared a "conspectus," or syllabus, of Yiddish for the students of the school divided into the following sections:

a. Brief history of Jewish languages
b. General history of Yiddish
c. Philological characteristics of Yiddish
d. Germanic element in Yiddish
e. Hebrew element in Yiddish
f. Slavic element in Yiddish
g. History of Yiddish lexicology
h. Yiddish grammar
i. Yiddish phonetics
j. Spelling
k. Main dialects
l. Literary language and pronunciation, aims of Yiddish philology and the teacher of Yiddish[18]

The curriculum at the four-, seven- and ten-year school, and at the Teachers' Seminaries and Jewish Sections or Departments of the various universities, clearly indicates that the Yiddish school was not merely a Soviet school in Yiddish. It was partly Jewish in content, for Yiddish literature, Yiddish language, and the history of the Jewish people were taught. The teaching in Yiddish was a nationalizing factor, and the works of Peretz, Sholem Aleichem, and Mendele Mokher Seforim surely added both Jewish content and Jewish values. It is true though that everything was taught from a narrow, Communist point of view, that the official slogan was national in form, socialist or proletarian in content, and that Yiddishism, Jewish Democratic Socialism, Bundism, Zionism, were attacked and denounced. The educational functionaries never wearied of repeating that the schools were national in form only, and they had no national aims and did not strive for national survival. But, in spite of these overt protestations, the schools did have a certain influence which implanted a Jewishness in the pupils that the Jewish children who did not go to the Yiddish schools did not possess.

The textbooks used, with their material from the Yiddish classics as well as by modern writers, added to this influence. The teaching of Jewish history, although it was framed as part of the history of Russia, or the Ukraine or Belorussia, did acquaint the children with some aspects of Jewish history, despite the Communist point of view.

These schools were not permitted to be reopened after the Second World War, because by that time the Soviet government had decided to enforce Stalin's and Lenin's views concerning the Jews—total and forced assimilation and integration with the majority population.

NOTES

1. *Tentative List of Jewish Educational Institutions in Axis-occupied Countries* by the Research Staff of the Commission on European Jewish Cultural Reconstruction. Supplement to Jewish Social Studies, Vol. VIII, No. 3 (July 1946), p. 93.

2. In 1936, I spent six weeks in the Soviet Union. I was in my native town, Slutsk, Belorussia, in Minsk, Kiev, Moscow, and Leningrad. I met Jewish youths, both those who graduated from Yiddish schools and those who studied at non-Jewish Soviet schools. One could note the difference immediately. Those who studied at Yiddish schools spoke Yiddish, knew Yiddish literature, read the Yiddish books, journals, and newspapers, attended the Yiddish theater, were interested in the Jews outside of Russia, and generally knew that they were Jews—whereas those who went to the non-Jewish language schools showed no interest in Jewish life at all.

3. *Di Bashtimung fun C.C.K.P.B. Vegn de Onfang un Mitl Shul* (The Decisions of the Central Committee of the All-Union Communist Party–Bolsheviks and Communist Party of Belorussia on the Elementary and Secondary School), Belorussian Government Publishing House, Minsk, 1931, pp. 1, 2, 3, 45.

4. I. Dardak, *op. cit.,* Chapter VII, note 19, pp. 177–179.

5. S. Klitenik, *Di Kultur Arbet tsvishn di Yidishe Arbetndike inem Ratn-Farband* (The Cultural Work Among the Jewish Toilers in the Soviet Union), Moscow, 1931, p. 11.

6. M. A. Skrypniak in *Ratn-Bildung,* No. 3–4, 1932, p. 24.

7. *Ratn-Bildung*, No. 1–2, 1932.
8. *Ratn-Bildung*, No. 4, July–August, 1934.
9. I. Dardak, *op. cit.*, p. 173.
10. *Program fun Yidish un Yidisher Literatur, I–VII* (Curriculum for Yiddish and Yiddish Literature), Minsk, 1925, pp. 3–4.
11. *Ibid.*, pp. 7–10.
12. *Ibid.*, pp. 11, 12, 13.
13. *Ibid.*, pp. 15–17.
14. *Program fun Yidish un Literatur far der Zibnyoriker Shul* (Curriculum for Yiddish and Literature for the Seven-Year School), Commissariat of Education, Minsk, 1927, pp. 3–6.
15. *Agliad* (Catalogue of Courses), University of Minsk, Minsk, 1926.
16. Dardak, *op. cit.*, p. 176.
17. *Visnshaftlekhe Yorbikhor I,* Central Publishing House for the Nationalities, Moscow, 1929, pp. 253–255.
18. M. Shpierayn, *Yidish, A Konspekt fun a Kurs in dem II Moskver Melukhishn Univerzitet.* Shul un Bukh, Yiddish, a Syllabus of a Course in the II State Moscow University, Moscow, 1926, p. 24.

CHAPTER 9

The Textbooks

AMONG the textbooks used in the Jewish-school system were Yiddish textbooks and those dealing with the social sciences, which included some Jewish history. Although in 1928 two pedagogues submitted a plan and a curriculum for teaching Jewish history four hours each week, and proposed that a textbook should be published incorporating their curriculum, their plan was not accepted and the proposed book was never published. The proposed curriculum would have included:

History of the Jews: to be taught in Grades V and VI

Grade V

Middle Ages: feudalization of Europe; arrival of Jews from Middle East and North Africa; emergence of Jewish settlements in Germany, France, Italy and Spain.

Occupations of the Jews, trades, business, pauperization, class divisions, agriculture.

Political and legal conditions in the Middle Ages. Ghettoes, communities.

Power of the synagogue.

Religious mystical character of Jewish culture in period of feudalism.

Participation of the Jews in the development of business capital.

Movement to Poland and Ukraine.

Jewish middlemen in Poland and Ukraine—between peasant, serf and landlord.

Grade VI

Jewish centers in the Ukraine.

Antagonism between Jews and non-Jews; national hatred on the base of social antagonism.

The division of Poland.

Jews in Russia; rise of industry.

Cultural life, emergence of Haskalah and Yiddish literature.

Jews in Russia in the second half of the nineteenth century.

Economic life, political life, Haskalah as the ideology of the Jewish bourgeoisie.[1]

Textbooks were made available for the study of mathematics, biology, physics, chemistry, and zoology. These books were written either by teachers of these subjects in the Yiddish schools, or they were translated from the Russian. Special terminologies for all the sciences were prepared by the scholars of the Institute for Jewish Proletarian Culture of the Ukrainian Academy of Science at Kiev, and by the Yiddish Sector of the Belorussian Academy of Science at Minsk.

The various science textbooks used in the Yiddish schools were of the same type as those used in the other schools in Soviet Russia. They all had to be approved by the People's Commissariat of Education. These scientific textbooks had no special significance for the Jewish school, as they were of the same type as those used in all the Russian schools, and therefore they will not be taken up here. The textbooks for Yiddish and Yiddish literature, used exclusively in the Yiddish schools, are important for our study.

Oktiaber Kinder (Children of October) is the name of a reader for the first year compiled by the students of the Jewish Pedagogical Tekhnikum of Minsk and edited by Kh. Holmshtok, L. Mishkovsky, S. Rives, I. Bakst, and N. Shulman. Approved by the Government Council for Elementary Schools, it was published by the Central Publishing House for the Nationalities of the U.S.S.R. in Moscow,

1926, and was reprinted in 1927. The reader had stories and poems by the non-Soviet writers Sholem Aleichem, Simon Frug, Mani Leib, Moshe Stavsky, and Y. L. Peretz, and also contained material by the Soviet writers Peretz Markish, Leib Kvitko, Khane Levine, Moishe Taitch and nonsigned material. The stories and poems were about school, and included illustrations of the classrooms with Lenin's picture on the wall; about nature; cleanliness and diligence are praised, and children were told how important it is to come to school on time.

A special section was devoted to "Our Calendar," opening with the date, January 21, 1924, when Lenin died. There were pictures of Lenin's funeral, the house where Lenin died, the Lenin Mausoleum, a Lenin corner in a school, and Lenin addressing a meeting, followed by a child's story, "I Saw Lenin." The concluding sections concern the Red Army, and the First of May, the international labor holiday. There is a picture of children marching and carrying signs with Yiddish inscriptions "Long Live the First of May" and "Workers of the World Unite." The reader has material about the little October children and the Pioneers, all candidates for the Communist Party. There was no Jewish content in this reader. The poems and stories by the non-Soviet writers were mostly about nature and domestic animals, but there were Hebrew words, idiomatic expressions, and the children all had popular Jewish names. Even the dogs and horses had Jewish names. There was also a selection from Sholem Aleichem's "Mottel, the Cantor's Son."

Yidish is the name of a textbook compiled by Eliahu Spivack published in 1923, by the Kultur Lige in Kiev, of which there were several editions. The contents of this book were Jewish, compared to the *Oktiaber Kinder*. The earlier a book was published, the more Jewish material it contained. The textbooks published later contain less Jewish material and the material included is especially selected to show the negative aspects of Jewish life under the Tsarist regime in Russia.

Spivack's *Yidish* of 1923 had poems and stories written for children on nonpolitical themes by both Soviet and non-Soviet writers, with Peretz and Sholem Aleichem among the most important. The story of Joseph, told well, even mentioned the word God. There was also Y. L. Peretz' translation of "Chad Gad'ya" and Mani Leib's "Ingl Tsingl Khvat." Most of the illustrations are by the great painter Eliezer Lissitski.

A comparison between *Yidish* and *October Children* shows the elimination of the Jewish element. While *Yidish* of 1922–23 contained an abundance of Jewish material, including a biblical story, *October Children* of 1926–27 was nearly devoid of any Jewish material and Soviet material predominates.

Arum Undz (Around Us) was a textbook intended for the second grade, compiled by Eliahu Spivack and published in Kiev in 1927. On the title page it bore the inscription: "Approved by the Scientific Committee of Education of the Ukrainian Socialistic Soviet Republic." In the introduction, the author stated that the textbook was merely to help the teacher organize his classwork, and should not in any way be a substitute for the work of the children themselves and their own daily experience. There were stories and poems by Y. L. Peretz, Sholem Aleichem, David Einhorn, Itzhak Katzenelson, Mani Leib, Morris Rosenfeld, Zalman Shneur, Abraham Reisen, Moshe Stavsky, Mendele Mokher, Seforim and other pre-Soviet writers. The text also contained stories and poems by the Soviet Yiddish writers Peretz Markish, Izy Kharik, Leib Kvitko, Itzik Feffer, Ezra Fininberg, David Hofshtein, and Noah Lurie, mostly about nature, the home, the farm, and the factory. There was an abundance of material about Communism, Lenin, and other revolutionary leaders such as Rosa Luxemburg and Karl Liebknecht. One poem is about the Pioneers, children who are being prepared for the Young Communist League:

> We are still
> And are still
> Little children.
> We are still learning
> And are learning now.
> But we announce
> To all those who struggle:
> We are ready
> We are ready
> To come and take our place.

Material about "Little Octobers" (Oktiaberlakh) who are pre-Pioneer age, includes their laws and regulations. The Oktiaberlakh help the Pioneers, the Young Communists, the Communists, the workers, and peasants.

"The Oktiaberlakh strive to become Young Pioneers."

"The Oktiaberlakh watch out for the cleanliness of their bodies and clothes."

"The Oktiaberlakh love to work."

This is followed by the questions:

"How many Oktiaberlakh are there in your class? In your school?"

"How were the Oktiaberlakh drawn into the organization? How do the elder comrades, the Pioneers, work among you?"

A special section was devoted to a description of a cooperative store, of how it contained the merchandise and how goods were distributed. This was followed by a section on the October Revolution. Stories told about what went on in the Smolny Institute, the headquarters of the Communist Party, and about the fighting. Poems about the Civil War preceded a dramatization with the following recitations:

First Group—Workers:
The Revolution destroyed our chains.
Second Group—Peasants:
The Revolution gave us land and freedom.
Third Group—Workers and Peasants:
The Revolution united us.
Group of children:
We, free children, now have a new school.
A Group of Women:
The Revolution has liberated us from slavery.

The Pioneer Hymn and the "Internationale" were then sung. The textbook described the school shop, how a house is built, how central heating is installed. Then there was a section devoted to the year 1905, the year of the first Revolution, a biography of Lenin, and a quotation from Lenin: "The course that the Soviet government has taken up can be accomplished only when millions of workers and peasants will participate." Special attention was paid to the German revolutionaries, Rosa Luxemburg and Karl Liebknecht, and to the Ukrainian national poet and revolutionary, Taras Shevchenko. The Paris Commune of 1871 was not forgotten, and there was a story, "A Mother of a Communard Speaks."

Jewish material is available in both the stories and poems of the pre- and post-revolutionary Yiddish writers. Life in a Jewish village was described, and there were stories about the anti-Jewish pogroms of the "white" generals.

Yidishe Shprakh (Yiddish Language) by the same author, Eliahu Spivack, published in Kiev in 1928, dealt with intonation, phonetics, orthography, and elements of morphology. Stories, poems, and articles imbued with the Bolshevik spirit and propaganda illustrated the rules of grammar. There was material about the club of the Pioneers and of the Young Communist League, again about the October Revolution, about workers' meetings and, in defiance of religious tradition, about farms and "Chazeyrimlach" (little pigs). The pupils were told to punctuate this paragraph (page 22):

> Step by step the working class marched [stepped] to the day of October—through blood and sacrifices. And here red flags shine and children awake, the workers achieve, and everything lives. A storm sweeps the world and goes through Poland, Germany, and Bulgaria, and all over. Here in our land stars shine, red banners, masses march toward a new life. Music, speeches, worlds, boats, seas, birds, trees—everything in red flame.

Undzer Vort (Our Word), published in Kiev in 1929, is a reader also written by Eliahu Spivack. It consisted of two parts, the first for pupils in the second year, and the second part for those in the third year.

The first part of the reader is divided into the following sections:

"Summer"
"Autumn, Autumnal Nature, Harvest"
"Back to School"
"October Revolution"
"Winter"
"Days to Remember"
"Spring"
"May Day"

The section "October Revolution" opened with the slogans: "Long live the Soviet Government! Workers of the world unite!" This was followed by the questions: "How and why did the workers and peasants fight for freedom and rights? Who are the Oktiaberlakh and Young Leninists–Pioneers? What do the Pioneers have to do when they grow up? What did the October Revolution give to the workers and peasants?" A guide was then presented for an October celebration in the school.

"Days to Remember" opened with a description of Lenin's childhood, followed by a story about his death.

"May Day" had instructions for celebrating the holiday; the children were assigned a composition on how the workers celebrated May Day in pre-Revolutionary Russia. The reader contained poems about the Red Army, about visits to farms and factories, and a story about the shop in the school. The language was simple and idiomatic, but there was no Jewish content.

The second part of the reader was divided into the same sections, with the stress on work in factories and farms, with stories about cooperatives and transportation. In a few stories the word "Jews" occurred, such as: "My father is a good-looking Jew, he has a nice face and a square black beard" (p. 43). There is also a description of a group of "idn-schmidn" (Jews-blacksmiths), but non-Jewish and Communist material is prevalent.[2]

Literarishe Khrestomatie (A Literary Anthology), a reader for the fifth and sixth grades, was compiled by G. Yabrov and published by the Government Publishing House of Belorussia in Minsk in 1926. The textbook listed the following sections:

I. The Village
   A. The old village
   B. The village after the Revolution
   C. The Jewish farm dweller *(Yeshuvnik)*
   D. The Jewish farmer in the Soviet Union
   E. The Jewish farmer in the United States

II. The *Shtetl*
   A. The Jewish *shtetl* in the first half of the nineteenth century
   B. The Jewish *shtetl* after the Revolution

III. The City
   A. The Jewish bourgeoisie and the *Luftmentch*
   B. The Jewish worker and independent toiler in small industry
   C. The Jewish worker and artisan after the Revolution
   D. The worker in heavy industry
   E. Growth of the city
   F. Hymn to work.

The most important pre-Revolutionary Jewish writers were represented by stories and poems in this reader: Abramovitch-Mendele, Sholem Aleichem, Y. L. Peretz, Sholem Asch, David Einhorn, Joseph Opatoshu, Zevi Hirshkan, I. M. Weissenberg, I. J. Singer, David Kassel. Both the negative and, to some degree, the positive aspects of Jewish life in pre-Revolutionary Russia were presented to the student. There was also a great deal of reading matter by the Soviet Yiddish writers including Markish, Hofshtein, Kharik, Feffer, Haim Gildin, and the Soviet Hebrew-Yiddish poet, Elisha Rodin. In the poems of the Soviet Yiddish poets certain passages derisively portray Jewish life in pre-Revolutionary Russia. Itzik Feffer writes in his poem, "My *Shtetl"*:

A muddy stream runs like Bialik's muddy tears,
An old man sits and sighs reading the crying Frug [Simon Frug];
On the main avenue Pioneers march
And in the market place Young Communists sing.

A reviewer criticized this textbook for including "immoral materials," such as "and empty is today her house, like her thin breasts" (Feffer); or for a story by Sholem Asch who wrote: "The world has thrown off its night clothes . . . and, with the smile of a bride that wakes up after the first night of her wedding, she smiled." This material was judged by the reviewer to be unfit for children of fifth and sixth grades.[3] As a whole, this reader was full of material about Jewish life, though the improvements after the Revolution are stressed.

Yidn af Erd is the name of a reader by I. and M. Greenberg, published by the Central Publishing House for the Nationalities of the U.S.S.R., Moscow, 1930, carrying the imprimatur of the Pedagogical Section of the Government Council for Science for Schools of the first four grades. The reader was divided thus:

I. A Jewish *Shtetl* Before [the Revolution]
II. The Condition of the Peasants
III. Government Officials
IV. Years of War and Civil War

These four sections, as shown by some quotations, gave a dark picture of Jewish life under Tsarism, containing material by pre-Revolutionary Yiddish writers, as shown by some quotations. "In the overpopulated cities of the overpopulated Jewish Pale of Settlement, Jews were pressed in with iron rings"; "The bourgeoisie wanted to use the hands of the government and of bandits to drown the revolution with Jewish blood" (p. 48); and, "The Revolution destroys the old and on its ruins it builds a new life" (p. 62).

The second part contained the following sections and subsections:

  I. After the Revolution
      A. From the old ruins to a new life
      B. A new generation rises
      C. Far from the old homes
 II. In New Places to New Labor
      A. From the crowded Pale to new land
      B. In the steppes
      C. In Belorussia
      D. Birobidzhan
      E. City and village

The reader stressed the settlement of Jews on the farms, the help given to the Jewish settlers by the Soviet government, and it made the point that without the Revolution and the attention of the Soviet Government the Jews would still be in the overpopulated towns of the crowded Pale of Settlement.

Zai Greyt (Be Prepared) was a beginner's book published in 1932, compiled by P. Burganski.[4] On the title page there was the inscription, "Permitted by the Scientific Methodological Section of the Commissariat of Education as a textbook to be used in the Yiddish Schools; censor #20106, signed V-20-1932." The text opened with a picture of children carrying a placard that reads: "May the Soviet Government Live—All in School." Each section began with a letter of the alphabet. The letter "L" was introduced by "Lenin" and a picture of Lenin. The letter "R" was introduced by a child painting a sign which read: "Arop dem Rov" (Down with the Rabbi), "Arop dem Rebn" (Down with the Rebbe [Khasidic Rabbi]). The letter "S" was introduced with a picture of Lenin and Stalin with the following lines:

> Lenin and Stalin are our leaders.
> Lenin and Stalin are the leaders of the All-Union Communist Party.
> Stalin is Lenin's best pupil.
> Stalin is the best Communist (p. 39).

The entire book, designed for children of the first grade, was full of Communist propaganda, of which the following is typical:

Enemies

Today we made these placards:
"Our enemies are
The Kulaks [rich peasants]
The Rabbi
The Priest
The Bourgeoisie
The capitalists of all countries
Fight against them" (p. 60)

This was accompanied by pictures showing a rabbi with a talit-bag in his hand, with a skull cap and a menorah in the background. The capitalist wore a high hat and held a bag with a dollar sign.

Ershte Trit (First Steps), a reader for Grade II, was compiled by E. Aleksandrove and T. Bensman and was published in 1932.[5] It, too, bears on the title page the legend that it was "permitted by the People's Commissariat of Education of Belorussia." The text was simple, the stories and poems readable. The entire content concerns Lenin, Stalin, factories, collective farms, the Red Army, the October Revolution, the five-year plans, and Soviet construction. There were boxed slogans which read:

All to the aid of the spring sowing.

More machines, more collective farms, is the directive of the Party.

Long live Bolshevist sowing (p. 48).

There are anti-religious slogans:

Don't celebrate Passover. Passover is the holiday of the rabbis and the bourgeoisie.

Nobody must be absent from our school on Passover.

Not one machine, not one workshop should be stopped.

In the days of Passover, help the spring sowing.

Expel the religious person, the kulak [rich peasant] and their God from the collective farm and from the factory (p. 63).

We challenge the children of the Belorussian school. The Belorussian children will not celebrate Easter, they will not go to church. We will exchange visits (p. 65).

Today we had a meeting in our school. We discussed Passover. The children all promised not to eat matzoh and to work during the holiday as always (p. 64).

No old, foolish holidays, our holidays are all new, proletarian.

Against matzoh, against the seder, against Passover clothes.

In our school no one must be absent.

Down with the old rust; down with God in the sky (p. 65).

In Kamf (In Struggle) was a reader and workbook for the third year, published by the Central Publishing House, Ukrainian Branch, Kharkov, 1930, and written by A. Makagan, L. Mishkovsky, E. Spivack, and Henach Kozakevitch. It was approved by the People's Commissariat of Education of the Ukraine. The material told of Pioneers, Young Communists and Communists, and Communist campers. One story about child labor in the United States was included, which told about the law that children under fourteen years of age were not allowed to work in the United States. It stated that, although inspectors were supposed to enforce these laws, thousands of young children were doing the hardest work both in factories and the fields. The story concluded: "Only the revolutionary part of the working class, under the leadership of the Communist Party, conducts the fight against child labor. The exploitation of children will last, until power in America is transferred to the workers and farmers" (p. 10).

Leienbukh (Reader) is the title of another primer for the first year, compiled by P. Burganski, and published in 1936. It was approved by the Commissariat of Education.[6] Its simple tales were about Lenin, his childhood, the Communist Party, Stalin, nature, animals, "chazerimlekh" (little pigs), collective farms, collective farmers, the Red Army, General Voroshilov, factories, and tractors. Boxed slogans were: "Long live Stalin," and "There is no room on the collective farm for the lazy ones" (p. 45). A typical poem read:

Once upon a time it was like this,
For landlords and kulaks, fields and estates,
For poor peasants sticks and whips.
They worked hard in the fields
And suffered hunger during the winter.
The landlords and kulaks were thrown out and power seized.
The Bolsheviks led us in the struggle and in battle
The landlords and kulaks were expelled.
And now we *are* free
We *are* building now collectives,
We *are* building a new life.

Another text entitled *Leienbukh* for the years II and III was compiled by Nahum Oyslender and published in 1936.[7] This text had many poems and stories by various writers, both Jewish and non-Jewish, pre-Revolutionary and post-Revolutionary. The stories were about Lenin, Stalin, collective farms, factories, the Red Army. A few stories by David Bergelson and Sholem Aleichem were included, but they presented a dark picture of pre-Revolutionary Jewish life. Those stories, as well as those by Mendele Mokher Seforim and Y. L. Peretz, were selected to show how terrible life was under Tsarism. Although the Communist propaganda was obvious, it was not as direct and vulgar as in the other primers previously described.

Literatur by I. Ravin and V. Shatz, a text for the fourth year, was published in 1933 in Minsk.[8] The reader contained a section of pre-October literature, with text mostly by the Yiddish writers Mendele, Sholem Aleichem, Peretz, Morris Vinchevsky, David Edelshtadt, I. Bovshover, and Bergelson. There was also material by the French writer, Victor Hugo, the Belorussian, Yanku Kupolo, and the Ukrainian, Taras Shevchenko. The selections were, apparently, selected to present a dark picture of both Jewish and non-Jewish life under capitalism. Soviet literature was represented by both Yiddish and non-Yiddish writers; among the latter were Panferov, Aleksandrovitch, and N. Krupskaya. There were conventional poems about Lenin, recollections of Lenin, songs about the Red Army, factories, and collective farms. Their purpose was to show how much more happily the people lived in the Soviet Union. In a section "Proletarian Literature in the Capitalist Countries," there was a poem "Comintern" by Miller, a story, "The

Strikers," by Kurt Kleber, and a poem, "Song of the Negro Shoe Shiner" by the American Yiddish writer, Moishe Shifris. The book concluded with the "Internationale."

Literarishe Khrestomatie (A Literary Anthology) by A. Holdes and P. Shames, a reader for the seventh year, was published in 1934.[9] The pre-Soviet Yiddish literature was presented by selections from David Bergelson's novels *Nokh Alemen* (After All) and *Bam Dnieper* (Near the Dnieper). Soviet Yiddish literature was represented by poems and stories about Lenin by M. Khachevatzky, collectivization by Note Lurie, factories by Haim Gildin, and Soviet construction by Peretz Markish, David Hofshtein, H. Orland, Itzik Feffer.[10] There was a special section, "Soviet Literature of the Nationalities," with translations from Belorussian and Ukrainian. Another section was devoted to contemporary foreign literature, with translations of poems about Lenin from the Hungarian, and stories by German Communist writers. The one Yiddish writer, Ziskind Lev, was represented by a story about Ukrainian peasants who lived in Poland.[11]

Gramatik un Ortographie (Grammar and Orthography) was a grammar text for the first two years, written by Isaac Zaretsky and published in 1934.[12] Among the texts used to illustrate certain grammatical rules, these are characteristic:

(Lenin)
In each region, in each land
Is his name known,
All over, wherever you go
You will see Lenin's picture (p. 5).

(Red Banner)
Waving in the air
Red it is as fire.
Us, children of October,
It is dear and beloved (p. 28).

(Against Religion)
The farmers of the collective farm "Neye Erd" work hard. They are harvesting, they are putting seed and food away for winter use. They are preparing food for the animals.

On the eve of Yom Kippur, the rabbi of the neighboring town came down to the collective farm. The rabbi approached every peasant and asked him to come to the synagogue. Not one of the peasants paid attention to the rabbi. Everyone worked during Yom Kippur in the garden (pp. 34–35).

(Slogans)
The October Revolution has thrown out the landlords and the cap-
italists.
The Soviet government is the government of workers and peas-
ants.
Comrade Stalin is Lenin's best pupil.
Long live the October Revolution!
Long live the Soviet government!
Long live the Communist Party!
Long live Comrade Stalin! (p. 49)

Another grammar textbook, by Khaim Loytsker and M. Shapiro,
was published in Kiev, 1940.[13] Among the materials used to
illustrate certain grammatical rules, here is a characteristic text:

> In 1917 the nationalities of the U.S.S.R. deposed the bourgeoisie,
> instituted the dictatorship of the proletariat, and organized the So-
> viet government. This is a fact, not merely a promise.
> When the Soviet government had expropriated the class of capi-
> talists, it gave to the peasants 150 million hectares of land that be-
> longed to private landlords, the government and the monasteries.
> This is besides the land that formerly belonged to the peasants. This
> is a fact, not a promise.
> After the Soviet government expropriated the capitalists, took
> away from them the banks, the factories, the railroads and other
> means of productions, and declared them as socialist property, they
> put at the head of these industries the best people of the working
> class. This is a fact, and not a promise.
>
> Stalin (p. 47)

Other texts deal with the life of Lenin (p. 104). But there
are a few excerpts from Itzik Feffer (p. 141), Note Lurie (p. 142),
and Sholem Aleichem (p. 143), which deal with Jewish subjects.
 Yidish is the name of a handbook which dealt with grammar,
phonetics and orthography, written by Elie Falkowitch, a well-
known grammarian.[14] All the examples were taken from Soviet
writing of which the following is typical (p. 204):

> The crisis in the capitalist world keeps on developing. Unemploy-
> ment grows. Hunger and poverty are spreading. Capitalism be-
> comes more militant, and it attacks the positions that were acquired
> by the working class. The establishment of a Fascist dictatorship in
> Germany has made clear to the workers the necessity for establish-
> ing a United Front to fight the Fascist aggression of the bourgeoisie.

When the textbooks dealing with the social studies are examined, it is noticeable that in the books published in the late twenties, the attitude toward the Jews and Jewish problems was "soft"; but it hardened around 1930, and Jewish history was then examined from a narrower, party point of view. As mentioned, the history of the Jewish people was not taught as a separate subject, but as part of world history.

Gezelshaftkentenish (Social Studies) was a textbook published in 1928, whose authors were I. Rubin, Z. Khanutin, L. Holmshtok, H. Aleksandrov, and I. Dardak.[15] The textbook dealt with the history of Western Europe, the rise of commerce and industry, the struggle between peasants and landlords, and early history of Belorussia and Lithuania. Chapters on the ghetto (pp. 47–48), and the Jews in Belorussia and Lithuania (pp. 94–104) were included. The authors told of how the Jews were forced into the ghetto, how the Christian competitors kept them there and how these competitors, with the aid of the priests, incited the Christians against the Jews (pp. 47–48). In a long chapter about the Jews in Belorussia and Lithuania, the authors stressed that the wealthy Jews suffered less than the Jewish artisans (p. 97); the guilds persecuted the Jewish artisans and workers (p. 100). The text described the activities of the Kehilah: (p. 102):

> The *Kahal,* through the *Melamdim,* rabbis and preachers *(magidim)* kept the plain people in fear and darkness, and saw to it that the Jews should be good and observant; it discouraged them from fighting against the wrongs committed by the rich, and they [were instrumental in keeping] the Jews . . . obedient as lambs that can be shorn endlessly.

A standard history text, *History: The Pre-Class Society, the Ancient East, the Antique World,* by academician N. M. Nikolski, was published in 1934. It was translated from the Russian by Uri Finkel. This textbook, written from an extreme Marxist point of view, was used in all Russian schools, but the Yiddish translation which was made for the Yiddish-language schools contained a few paragraphs written specially for this edition by N. M. Nikolski.[16] The specially written chapters were "Israel and Judea" (p. 87), "The Feudal System of Israel and Judea" (p. 88), "The Feudal Religion" (p. 90), "Class Struggle in Israel and Judea" (p. 91), "Religion and Its Fight against the Peasant Revolution" (p. 92).

The section about the Jews in the ancient world was also written
from the same viewpoint. One paragraph serves to illustrate this
(p. 90):

The present-day servants of the Jewish religion, the rabbis, say
that the Jewish religion is a special one that is not similar to other
religions. All nations, the rabbis say, were polytheistic—but the
Jews were, from the very beginning, monotheistic. Therefore, they
say, the Jewish religion is the most complete and the truest religion
in the world.

All these claims by the rabbis and clergy are lies and aim to fool
the people. All religions are the same, all are permeated with lies
and foolishness. And gods—it does not matter whether people
count one God or many gods—do not exist, they are only a product
of the human imagination. These are invented and not real beings.
But the rabbis tell lies and fool the Jews, when they say that the
Jewish religion is not similar to other religions, because the Jews
were supposed to be monotheists from the very beginning. This is
simply not true. The Jewish religion was like all other religions—it
came through the same road as the others.

And here is a statement about the prophets (p. 93):

The prophets usually told the peasants that their complaints and
sighs have reached God and God will soon send a redeemer; one
must have patience and fulfill the commandments of the priests, that
the Gods may not be angered and, thus, not send the redeemer. This
redeemer, the prophets usually said, will be a king, beloved by the
Gods. In the second half of the eighth century, with such promises,
a prophet by the name Isaiah, tried to divert the peasants from the
class struggle. . . . Isaiah added that, at present, no rebellions should
be staged, no protests made, but celebrations should be arranged to
celebrate the future birth of the king.

In the pedagogical institutes, Nikolski's two other works were
used. The first, *Ancient Israel,* was published in 1919–1920; the
second, *Jewish Holidays,* was published in 1925.[17] *Ancient Israel,*
because of its earlier publication, is free from Communist or even
Marxist interpretations. The book was written from the point of
view of higher Biblical criticism, but in a more positive tone. In
the first chapter the author stated that the once mighty neighbors
of the Jews, the Egyptians, the Babylonians, the Assyrians, had
all disappeared, stone tablets their only reminder. The Jewish
people, however, remained alive and "the best literature of the

ancient Israelites was preserved and is known to the whole world—the Bible—a book that is sacred both to Jews and Christians" (pp. 4–5). Nikolski further stated: "We can't remain indifferent to the history of such a people, too many threads tie us to the past of the Jewish people" (p. 5). Nikolski concluded his book with the destruction of the first Temple (p. 277):

> It is possible that it may be only a dream, that the Messiah will never come, and the Jewish people will always remain in the Diaspora. But we must admit that it was a great nation that created an original culture, and its sufferings were as great, even greater than Job's, and for these sufferings it deserved a better life than it has now.

Jewish Holidays, by the same author, was published in 1925. In the five or six years that passed since the publication of his *Ancient Israel,* the political climate had changed in Russia, and Nikolski passed from higher Biblical criticism to Marxism and began to consider his work as part of the antireligious campaign. His introduction clearly showed this (p. 1):

> In the daily life of the contemporary Jew, religious superstition still plays an important part—especially the religious holidays. . . . Even now many Jews, on the Sabbath, become simply slaves of religious dogmas. Not only do these people not work on the Sabbath, but they even refuse to attend to the daily necessities; thus they don't make a fire, and don't cook. As in ancient times, the Jews still observe the Passover, with its matzohs. The rabbis especially see to it that the holidays should be observed. The reason is simple: because the main thing in religion is not faith, but its practical aspects, to observe the laws, fulfill the commandments, to fast, and to participate in all the ceremonies that are connected with religion.

Nikolski applied the "scientific" Marxist approach to show the economic and political factors in the development of the Jewish holidays. He also argued that the aim of the Jewish holidays was to dull the class-consciousness of the Jewish workers. The only holidays they should observe were the proletarian holidays (pp. 151–152). He concluded his book with a quotation from the "Internationale" (p. 154):

> No one will liberate us
> No God, not a hero
> With our own arms
> We bring salvation.

Although this book was more militant, more Marxist, and more filled with party antireligious propaganda than his "Ancient Israel," it was much less slanted than the reader for Grade V that was discussed before. Nikolski followed the party line, as did everyone else in Russia, and his three books, which were used in the Jewish schools, show how it influenced his opinion of Jewish values in the Jewish schools.

Textbooks and selections of the earlier Yiddish literature were made available to students of the teachers' seminaries. The selections and texts had introductions by the editors and compilers which helped the students and teachers to understand the literature of the period. *Di Eltere Yidishe Literatur* (The Older Yiddish Literature) was the name of a volume prepared by Naḥum Shtif.[18] It presented the writings of Itzhak Baer Levinsohn, Shloyme Etinger, Israel Aksenfeld, Isaac Meier Dick, Michael Gordon, Shmuel Bernstein, Judah Leib Gordon, Beryl Broder, Wolf Erenkrantz, Itzhak Joel Linetsky, and Abraham Goldfadn. Shtif's introduction was written from a secular, Yiddishist point of view, and he was taken to task for it.[19]

Yidishe Literatur, an anthology of literature and criticism was published in Kiev, 1928. It was compiled by Naḥum Oyslender, D. Volkenshtein, N. Lurie and Ezra Fininberg.[20] The text was prepared for the students of the upper grades of the school as well as for the students of the Pedagogical Tekhnikums (Teachers' Institutes), and covered Yiddish literature from about 1860 to the first Russian Revolution in 1905. A second part, embracing the literature from 1905 to the end of the twenties, was planned but never published.

In the brief introduction, the authors stated that they utilized only those materials that harmonized with the demands of socialist pedagogy. The editor of the volume, M. Levitan, stated that although Yiddish literature was oriented to the workers and toilers and the poorest section of the Jewish people, "whose interests fit within the proletarian ideology," the literature was created by the intelligentsia, ideologically near the petit bourgeoisie and even the upper middle class. Therefore, the Yiddish writer was caught between two opposing ideologies. The writer was ideologically from the middle class, yet he wrote for an audience that was opposed to the middle class and its ideals. One of the aims of the textbook was to point out this contradiction. The textbook stressed the class influences on the literature of the period it covered, and put into focus the revolutionary trend in the literature that was represented by the revolutionary Yiddish poets. The book was really an anthology of literary historical studies and literary criticism. It began with various essays and studies of Jewish life in the nineteenth century, both in Europe and America, followed by a number of other essays.

Among the contributors were the Soviet writers Moshe Litvakov, M. Raffress, I. Sosis, Oyslender, and the non-Soviet writers S. Niger and Jacob Lestschinsky. (Israel Tsinberg, though he lived and wrote in Russia, was not considered a Soviet writer because he did not write according to the Soviet demands; but the book contains his essay about the Yiddish weekly, the *Kol Mevaser.*) The social element in the literature of the period was discussed by the Soviet critics and literary historians, and in the "questions and problems" which follow each writer, the editor and compiler stressed the ideology of the writer. There are special footnotes where the compilers again reiterated their special party view of literature and of the individual writers presented.

The Comedies of the Berlin Enlightenment was a textbook prepared for use in the Yiddish literature course in the Pedagogical Institutes.[21] It was edited and introduced by Max Erik. The volume consisted of Itzik Eikhel's *Reb Henakh, or What Should be Done With It,* and Aaron H. Wolfsohn's *Superficiality and Hypocrisy.* Both plays were written in the eighteenth-century Yiddish. Eikhel's play was translated into modern Yiddish by David Hofshtein, and Wolfsohn's play was given both in the original Yiddish of the eighteenth century and in a modern translation by Hofshtein.

The editor, Max Erik, stated in the introduction that both plays were the first two Jewish bourgeois comedies, and their authors expressed the enlightened ideology of the rising Jewish bourgeoisie. He then analyzed the Haskalah from a Marxist point of view and related the two authors to the Haskalah movement in Germany.

An important textbook for the pedagogical institutes was *The Selected Works* of Solomon Etinger (1801–1856).[22] The book was edited and contained an introduction by Max Erik, in which he stated:

> In Etinger's fables his class ideology is very clear, his whole outlook upon life is evident, and his ideology bourgeois, and very lim-

ited. Etinger's moralizing does not rise above the limited, bourgeois philosophy. . . . The self-satisfied, provincial [character] of the bourgeoisie is evident. . . . In Etinger's works there is no opposition to absolutism. The King that is personified in a lion, is an enlightened monarch, who governs with a strong arm, but with justice to his subjects. . . . In the fable "Shmates," there is an energetic defense of the Tsarist recruiting program. The fearful Tsarist recruiting into the army, is described as an idyl, and Etinger's position is more to the right than Aksenfeld's and Levinsohn's.

Etinger's classic play *Serkele* was characterized by Erik as a bourgeois comedy, which later served as a model for the dramatic works of Abraham Goldfadn and Sholem Aleichem (p. 33).

The works of Israel Aksenfeld (1787–1866) that survived, were collected and edited for the use in the Teachers' Institutes. Aksenfeld's *Verk* (Works) were edited by Meier Winer, who wrote the usual introduction about the bourgeois nature of Aksenfeld's writings. Aksenfeld's sharp criticism of the Hasidim was analyzed and, naturally, approved.[23]

Yiddish Literature in the XIX Century was a textbook for the teachers' seminaries. The authors were Max Erik and A. Rozenzweig. Erik wrote a general introduction and the first five chapters about I. B. Levinsohn, Israel Aksenfeld, Solomon Etinger and Abraham Ben Gottlober. Rozenzweig wrote about Linetsky and Mendele-Abramovitch.[24] A second volume, covering the classical period, was promised but never appeared.

The book was written from a Marxist point of view, which showed the influence of the political and economic factors upon literature. Erik emphasized the bourgeois character of the Haskalah and in his analysis of the Haskalah writers attempted to prove how limited they were by their bourgeois outlook. He criticized Levinsohn, who believed in the goodwill of the Tsar, advised not to fight the rabbis, and based his Haskalah philosophy on rabbinical sources; and showed that enlightenment was a product of normative Judaism. Erik praised Levinsohn for expressing sympathy for the poor and for his sharp criticism of contemporary Jewish life. Erik took Gottlober to task for, though he wrote well about the life of the period, he lacked an ideology or any original ideas. Rozenzweig analyzed both the minor and major writings of those Jewish writers who wrote in Russian, and the effectiveness of populist writers like J. M. Lifshitz. He was especially enthusiastic about Linetsky, who in his book, *Dos Poylishe Yingl* (The Polish Boy), attacked contemporary Jewish life. In his chapter on Mendele Mokher Seforim, the author criticized him for not understanding the events of his time, for his lack of knowledge of the class struggle, and for his failure to solve the Jewish problem. In other words, Rozenzweig criticized Mendele Mokher Seforim-Abramovitch for not being a Communist, and for not propagandizing communism in his *Fishke the Cripple* or the *Magic Ring*.[25]

In conclusion, it becomes clear that the readers that were published in the early twenties contained a great deal of Jewish material, and were less critical of Jewish life. But by the end of the twenties the new readers possessed less and less Jewish content, and the material selected gave a dark picture of Jewish life before the October Revolution. In the readers published in the thirties, the Jewish content decreased and was replaced by the open Communist and anti-religious propaganda. Even in grammars and handbooks about style, the samples to illustrate rules or forms of style, were taken from contemporary Communist documents.

The same is true of the books on social studies, where some material about history was included. In the textbooks published in the late twenties the authors displayed some understanding of the Jewish past, while in the history textbooks published in the thirties, the material was focused to fit the Stalinist point of view. The class struggle, in the Jewish milieu, was emphasized, and the Jewish religion was treated as a tool in the hands of the rich who, aided by the rabbis, oppressed the poor. The textbooks of the thirties give a good picture of the complete Stalinization of the Yiddish-language school.

The textbooks on literature went through the same process. Those published in the late twenties had mildly Marxist introductions, while those that were published in the thirties had introductions that stressed the bourgeois character of Yiddish literature and the limitations of the writers. The introductions stressed the class conflicts in Jewish life and the "reactionary" role played by the Hasidic movement. The Haskalah movement and its literature were criticized. While the textbooks gave the students an opportunity to study Yiddish literature, the introductions completely distorted its real value, meaning, and significance. Despite these distortions, the students did learn Yiddish literature and they acquired some knowledge about Jewish life.

NOTES

1. L. Strizhak and A. Buzhewitch, *Program far Lernen Yidishe Geshikhte* (Outline for Teaching Jewish History), *Ratn-Bildung*, No. 3, 1928, Kiev.

2. Eliahu Spivack was arrested in November 1948 and executed with a number of other Jewish writers, in August 1952. *A Shpigl Oyf a Steyn*, an anthology of poetry and prose by twelve Soviet Yiddish writers. Edited with introduction and notes by Kh. Shmeruk. Tel Aviv, 1964, pp. 8–9.

3. *Ratn-Bildung*, No. 4, July–August 1928.

4. P. Burganski, *Zai Greyt*, Government Publishing House for the National Minorities, Kiev, 1932, p. 80.

5. E. Aleksandrove and T. Bensman, *Ershte Trit*, Government Publishing House of Belorussia, Jewish Sector, Minsk, 1932, p. 95.

6. P. Burganski, *Leienbukh*, I year, Government Publishing House for the National Minorities, Kiev, 1936, p. 108.

7. N. Oyslender, *Leienbukh*, Government Publishing House for the Minorities in Ukraine, Kiev, 1936, p. 128.

8. I. Ravin and V. Shatz, *Literatur*, a reader for the fourth year, certified by the Collegium of the People's Commissariat of Education in Belorussia, Government Publishing House of Belorussia, Minsk, 1933, p. 176.

9. A. Holdes and P. Shames, *Literarishe Khrestomatie*, Government Publishing House for the Nationalities, Kiev, 1934, p. 328.

10. David Bergelson, David Hofshtein, Peretz Markish, Itzik Feffer, were arrested November, 1948, and executed August, 1952. Haim Gildin died in a Siberian camp. See note 2.

11. Ziskind Lev settled in Russia, was arrested and executed as an "enemy of the people."

12. Professor I. Zaretsky, *Gramatik un Ortografie*, Part I, Government Publishing House for the National Minorities in the Ukraine, Kiev, 1934, p. 100.

13. Kh. Loytzker and M. Shapiro, *Gramatik*, Part I, "Morphology," for Grades V and VI, Government Publishing House for the National Minorities in the Ukraine, Kiev, 1940, p. 172; reprinted in Kovno, 1940.

14. E. Falkowitch, *Yidish*, Emes Publishers, Moscow, 1936, p. 327.

15. I. Rubin, Z. Khanutin, L. Holmshtok, H. Aleksandrov, and I. Dardak, *Gezelshaftkentenish*, Government Publishing House of Belorussia, Minsk, 1928, p. 106.

16. Academician N. M. Nikolski, *Geshikhte: Di Farklasndike Gezelshaft, der Uralter Mizrakh, di Antike Velt*, translated by Uri Finkel, Emes Publishing House, Moscow, 1934, p. 254.

17. N. M. Nikolski, *Dos Uralte Folk Israel* (Ancient Israel), Yiddish by A. Rosenthal, published by the Central Commissariat for Jewish Affairs, Moscow, 1919–1920, p. 279. N. M. Nikolski, *Yidishe Yomtoyvim, Zeyer Oyfkum un Antviklung* (Jewish Holidays, Their Origin and Development), translated into Yiddish by Kh. Maizel and Uri Finkel, Government Publishing House of Belorussia, Minsk, 1925, p. 154.

18. N. Shtif, *Di Eltere Yidishe Literatur* (The Older Yiddish Literature), Cooperative Publishing House Kultur Lige, Kiev, 1929, p. 284.

19. Max Erik, "Shtif's Haskalah Khrestomatie," *Shtern*, Minsk, No. 1, 1930.

20. N. Oyslender, D. Volkenshtein, N. Lurie, and Ezra Finenberg, *Yidishe Literatur,* a *khrestomatie* of literature and criticism, Part I, Cooperative Publishing House Kultur Lige, Kiev, 1928, p. 364. The second part never appeared.

21. *Di Komedies fun der Berliner Oyfklerung* (The Comedies of the Berlin Enlightenment), edited with an introduction by Max Erik, Government Publishing House for the National Minorities in the Ukraine, Kiev, 1933, p. 187.

22. S. Etinger, *Geklibene Verk* (Selected Works), edited by Max Erik, Press of the Ukrainian Academy of Sciences, Kiev, 1935, p. 388.

23. I. Aksenfeld, *Verk,* edited by Meier Winer, Government Publishing House for Literature and Art, Kiev, 1931, pp. 374. Meier Winer (1893–1941) was a Jewish scholar who, together with Khaim Brody, published the well-known anthology *Mivekhar ha'Shira ha'Ivrit,* 1922. He also wrote an essay, "Prophecy and Mysticism," 1918. In 1926 he became a Communist, settled in Russia, wrote a great deal about nineteenth-century Yiddish literature. He was killed in the battle of Moscow, 1941.

24. M. Erik and A. Rozenzweig, *Di Yidishe Literatur in XIX Yorhundert* (Yiddish Literature in the Nineteenth Century), Government Publishing House for the National Minorities in the Ukraine, Kiev, 1935, p. 300.

25. The present writer reviewed the book in the Yiddish weekly, *Literarishe Bleter,* No. 36, September 4, 1936, Warsaw, pp. 566–567.

CHAPTER 10

The Decline of the Schools

THE Yiddish-language schools reached their zenith in the early nineteen-thirties, followed by their decline and eventual liquidation. There were many factors that led to the dissolution of the schools, but primarily it was the government decision to apply Lenin's and Stalin's Jewish program—assimilation of the Jews.

The dissolution of the schools, as well as the gradual curtailment of all Jewish cultural activities, was heralded by the dissolution of the Jewish Sections of the Communist Party in March, 1930. On March 8, 1930, the Moscow daily, *Emes,* still carried on the masthead the following: "Organ of the Central Bureau of the Jewish Sections of the Central Committee of the All-Union Communist Party." A day later this inscription was replaced with the following: "Organ of the Nationalities' Council of the Central Executive Committee of the Union of Soviet Socialist Republics," thus eradicating the last vestiges of Jewishness.

The same issue of *Emes*[1] carried two leading articles: one was an unsigned editorial, and the other was signed by Simon Dimanshtein. The editorial read:

> The national work has outgrown the special organizational forms and it—the work—demands a more organized party task. There-

fore, a special office is now being formed of instructors for the national minorities at the Executive Committee of the Government of the U.S.S.R., to supervise the work among the national minorities throughout the Soviet Union. The Jewish work, both of the party and of the government, has developed, and direct government supervision is necessary.

Dimanshtein's article, printed on page one, column one, stated that the

> Party has given directives that all divisions of the Central Committee of the Communist Party, and the local organs of the Party must, each according to its task, handle the problems of the national minorities. It is pointed out that in no case should the work among the national minorities suffer because the National Sections of the Party are being liquidated.

Dimanshtein mentioned that in the work of national sections of the Communist Party there was a great deal of overlapping, parallelism, with other sections of the Central Committee. The dissolution of the Jewish sections of the Communist Party meant the abolition of inefficiency and duplication of work.

This, of course, was not the real reason for the liquidation of the Jewish Sections of the Communist Party. The real reason was stated two years later in the *Great Soviet Encyclopedia*. The statement says: "In order to overcome, once and for all, the national tendencies still observable in the activity of the Jewish Sections, the latter . . . were liquidated at the center as well as locally."[2]

The elimination of Jewish Sections of the Communist Party resulted in there being no Jewish organization to supervise the schools, to encourage parents to send their children to the Yiddish-language schools or to carry on propaganda for these schools. No Jewish group existed which could organize new schools, or oversee their development. The schools remained without parents, as a foreign visitor correctly observed.[3] The fate of the Jewish schools remained in the hands of the local Ukrainian, Belorussian, or Russian officials who showed interest in the schools only when it fitted their policies of Ukrainization or Belorussification.

Another reason for the decline of the Yiddish-language schools was the indifference, and often the hostility of the parents who had been accustomed to the religious hadorim. Prior to the Bolshevik seizure of power in November 1917, the vast majority of Jewish children attended the religious hadorim. In 1917, out of 400,000

Jewish children of school age, only about 30,000 attended Jewish secular schools with Russian as the language of instruction.[4] On the eve of the First World War, there were 8,942 hadorim with an enrollment of 325,000 children.[5] The transfer of the children from the extremely religious hadorim to the secular, atheistic, Communist, Yiddish-language schools was a traumatic experience both for the parents and the children. Many Jewish parents who struggled against these schools petitioned the Soviet government to allow them to send their children to hadorim. Thus in 1922, a group of parents in Smolensk, who petitioned the government to reopen the hadorim, wrote: "Taking into consideration the proclamation of religious freedom, we ask you to remove the obstacles and allow us to reopen the hadorim. The hadorim will function in the afternoon and will not interfere with the functioning of the regular schools."[6] Secret hadorim were found in various cities in Belorussia.[7] The parents were more willing to send their children to Russian schools, where the antireligious propaganda was more general and, unlike the Yiddish schools, not specifically directed against the Jewish religion. The parents also felt that the Russian schools gave the children greater opportunity than did the Yiddish-language schools.[8] Whereas the Yiddish-language-school graduates could continue at various Yiddish technical schools and become machinists, or enroll at various Yiddish pedagogical schools and become teachers, they could not study medicine or science or mathematics without passing extremely difficult entrance examinations for general universities. The children chose the Russian-language schools or Belorussian or Ukrainian, where they could enter universities upon their graduation. "It is more practical" (more *takhles*) to study at a Russian school, was the universal cry of the parents.[9]

M. Levitan, who was the director of the Bureau of Education of the Jewish Sections of the Communist Party before its dissolution, pointed out that in the census of 1926, 76 percent of the Jews in the Ukraine gave Yiddish as their language, but only 45.5 percent of the Jewish children of school age attended Jewish schools. The reasons why the majority of the Jewish children chose non-Jewish language schools were, according to Levitan:

> The opposition of the anti-Soviet Zionist and clerical groups who saw in the general Soviet school a lesser evil than in the Yiddish-language school.

The petit-bourgeois prejudice against Yiddish that was retained even among Jewish workers.

The fact that Yiddish had not occupied the position in the government to which it was entitled according to the principles of the Soviet policy.

The fact that the local authorities discriminated against the Yiddish schools and did not allow them sufficient funds for new buildings and renovations; the absence of Yiddish colleges and universities where the graduates of the Yiddish schools could complete their education.[10]

Levitan's reasons were valid, and it took the Jewish Communists and the Jewish sections of the Communist Party a great deal of time and work to put nearly 50 percent of the Jewish children into the Yiddish-language schools. Once the Jewish sections were dissolved, there was no organized Jewish body to work on behalf of the schools.

While there still were Jewish functionaries or instructors for the Jewish schools, they had to conduct a struggle on a double front. They struggled with the Jewish parents to send their children to the Yiddish-language schools, and yet they had to declare that they were not Yiddishists, or nationalists, but that they were merely carrying out the regulation that the children should receive a Soviet education in their mother tongue. Thus one Communist Jewish functionary declared:

> The conditions under which the Yiddish school grew, the struggle against the school that was conducted by the Zionists and by the plain people, who did not see any practical results from attending a Yiddish school and who wanted to unite the heder with the Russian school, forced the honest Yiddish teacher to participate actively in the struggle for the Yiddish school, and to fight the reactionary, dark forces that strove to destroy the Yiddish school. This forced the Yiddish teacher to recognize the Soviet government, the party leadership of the Jewish sections long before the Russian teachers, or the Ukrainian teachers became reconciled with the Soviet government. The teacher was the pioneer of Soviet Yiddish cultural work. Not only did he help to build and popularize the idea of the Yiddish school, but he participated actively in the fight against the heder, clericalism and Zionism.[11]

In their agitation for the Yiddish school, one Communist official, Tchemeriski, stated:

Cultural and educational work has to be conducted in Yiddish because it is the language of the majority of the Jewish population. Only then, when cultural work is conducted in Yiddish, will it fulfill its social function. This principle answers the problem about the language of the school for the Jewish child. It is therefore essential that the principle of the mother tongue should be enforced. In order to achieve this, it is necessary to conduct a systematic propaganda campaign to enforce this principle. The principle of the mother tongue in our cultural and educational work must be carried out not in a militant way, not in militant Yiddishist ways, but as a social function of our work.[12]

The Jewish functionaries were always on their guard against being accused of Jewish nationalism or Yiddishism, and they had to maneuver carefully to work for the expansion of the schools without being accused of nationalism.

M. Levitan, whom we quoted earlier, declared in 1932 that Soviet Jewish culture and all its branches were an organic part of the entire Soviet culture, but that Yiddish work in the Soviet Union was not a continuation of Yiddishism outside Russia. He condemned those who saw any link between Yiddish cultural work in the Soviet Union with Yiddishism or with the Yiddishists outside the country where Yiddishism had a "Fascist tendency." Levitan further stated:

Yiddishism from its very beginning was a petit-bourgeois, nationalistic, and democratic cultural movement. The Yiddishists introduced in the Yiddish schools Sholem Asch's stories from the Bible, Bialik and Ravnitsky's *Sefer Ha'agada,* Myerzohn's clerical history of the Jews, and they celebrated the Jewish holidays. The Yiddishists did not dare to throw out Hebrew from the schools.

But some may say that the Soviet Jewish cultural activity operates also with the same instrument as the Yiddishists do—with Yiddish. But what is to be drawn from the fact that both employ Yiddish? Absolutely not that which the idolizers and apologists of Yiddish wish to show. For us, what is important is not the identity of the language instrument, for us the importance lies in the content.

We conclude that the Soviet Jewish cultural construction is not a continuation nor is it a higher step from Yiddishism—but it is a continuation of the proletarian cultural work that was done until the October Revolution. We look upon our Jewish work as part of the whole international proletarian culture. The 160,000 pupils who study in the Soviet Yiddish schools must be enclosed within the frame with the twenty-three million children who study in the schools of the Soviet Union in all languages. The Yiddish pedagogical tekhnikums and branches at institutes must be put in the same frame of other tekhnikums where a million and a half students study.[13]

This constant fear of being accused of nationalism and Yiddishism prevented the Jewish Communist functionaries from realizing their early dream of Yiddishizing all the Jewish children and placing them in Yiddish schools. Even as late as 1932, there were some Jewish functionaries who spoke about having all Jewish children in Yiddish schools.[14] One functionary stressed that the pupils of the Yiddish schools were not the children of the poor nor of the de-classed, disfranchised elements. The Yiddish school was really a public school and the *shtetl*, with its graduates of the Yiddish schools, was changing in appearance from the traditional *shtetl*.[15]

There were two strong factors in favor of the Yiddish school: Many Jews still lived in the *shtetl* where Yiddish was the dominating language; and regional nationalism was strong in the Ukraine and in Belorussia. Urged by Jewish Communists, the Jewish parents would choose a Yiddish school over a Ukrainian or a Belorussian school. The central government started a campaign against the Ukrainian and Belorussian Communists, accusing them of nationalism, and crushed the national trends. When Russian schools began to expand in the two republics, the Jewish parents were permitted to send their children to them, the sharp decline of the Yiddish school began. The shift of the Jewish population from the small towns to the large industrial centers, where there was no pressure from the Jewish Communists for Yiddishization, contributed to the decline.[16]

In the early 1930's, the central government at Moscow carried out a program which centralized the economic, social, and cultural life of the various republics. Many of the non-Russian intelligentsia were purged, and replaced in their positions by Russians. The schools in the many republics had to teach everything within the framework of a pro-Russian orientation. In the Ukraine and Belorussia, forced Ukrainization and Belorussification was declared to be counterrevolutionary. By 1933, Ukrainization had disintegrated and many Ukrainian organizations and educational institutions lapsed in their use of the Ukrainian language and ceased to empha-

size its importance.[17] Forced Yiddishization was stopped as well.
Russian schools were opened in the Ukraine and Belorussia, which
had an immediate effect on the Yiddish schools. Three Yiddish
schools in Kiev closed in 1935 because the parents chose Russian-
language schools for their children.[18]

Stalin's campaign against the "forcible Ukrainization" as
advocated by the Ukrainian Communist leader, Skrypniak, resulted
in his suicide on July 7, 1933, and the abandonment of his policy.
At the opening session of the Seventeenth Party Congress of the
Communist Party (January 1934), Stalin summarized all the mistakes of the "nationalists." He declared that the nationalism of the
Ukrainians was more dangerous to Communism than Great Russian
chauvinism, and that the struggle against Ukrainian nationalism
required a more efficient battle.[19] The battle against general nationalism and against the spirit of Jewishness in the Yiddish-language
schools, as well as the emergence of Russian schools open to Jewish
children, precipitated the deterioration of the Yiddish schools.

Naturally, the Communist functionaries of the Jewish educational
institutions approved Stalin's decrees and pronouncements against
the various nationalistic deviations, and they applied them to the
Jewish milieu. A conference was called as early as December 1931
by the Institute for Jewish Proletarian Culture to discuss the activities of the teachers in the Yiddish schools. The conference actually
examined how well the Yiddish schools carried out the policy of
the central government concerning forced Yiddishization. The conference took into consideration the struggle against Ukrainian
nationalism, and applied it to the Yiddish schools.

At first, general principles of education were discussed. One of
the educational functionaries, I. Reznik, confessed that he struggled
against the old school and tried to introduce Marxist-Leninist
principles of education into the schools. The reason he did not
always succeed was because he could not liberate himself from the
petit-bourgeois influences which he propagandized.[20] The same
speaker condemned the educational functionary, Gorokhov, whose
opinion that the aim of education was to create an ethical personality, went back to 1922. This, Reznik said, harmonized with
the theories of the clerical-bourgeois pedagogy of Herbart.[21]

But the sharpest attack was directed against Yokhinson. Yokhinson, according to the speaker I. Reznik, presented anti-Marxist
and antiworking-class material "under the mask of objectivism."

When teaching cultural history, he spoke about the Bible, and later even mentioned Herzl and his Utopian novel *Alt-Neiland*. Yokhinson was accused of idealism, of mechanistically applying Marxism, misrepresenting the Marxist theory of inherited characteristics, and for wrongly defining "nationality." He was condemned for his opinion that Jewish children were different from non-Jewish children, and that he did not differentiate between Jewish children whose parents were poor, workers, and sugar manufacturers.[22]

The conference adopted a resolution to unmask all petit-bourgeois influences in the Yiddish schools, and to conduct an unrelenting struggle against "the Fascist pedagogical literature that is being published in Yiddish abroad."[23]

In this atmosphere of confessions and accusations that led to arrests and liquidations, the Yiddish schools could not function normally. The conference, with its general attack on nationalism, led to the weakening and closing of many schools, and to loud cries against forcible Yiddishization. Anti-Yiddishization was heralded by A. Makagan in a signed editorial in the journal *Ratn-Bildung:* "In the Yiddish-language press no proper battle was conducted against forcible Ukrainization and forcible Yiddishization. Both forcible Ukrainization and forcible Yiddishization were propagated."[24] The editor singled out and criticized a Yiddish teacher who fought against the closing of the Yiddish school, not because the Yiddish school constituted an important position for the Soviet government in its struggle against the influence of the clergy, but because: "here we have a demand for forcible Yiddishization, as late as 1931, under the veil of a struggle against the petit-bourgeois Jewish environment." Makagan in the same editorial advocated the teaching of more Russian in the Yiddish schools. He also understood "the prejudices of the parents in favor of the Russian-language school."

M. Levitan, who was then an "instructor" appointed by the party to supervise the Yiddish schools, published a statement about "Forcible Yiddishization and Yiddishizers."[25] "Forcible Yiddishization," he stated, expressed itself in a number of ways, among them the transfer from the Russian language to Yiddish, in schools where the Yiddish-speaking children constituted a small percentage of the total number of students. Groups of Jewish children, some of whom knew no Yiddish, were transferred from Russian and Ukrainian schools to Yiddish schools, against their parents' wishes.

Some schools were Yiddishized which contained non-Jewish pupils. Due to' negligence of the Party, a few fanatic Yiddishist teachers created a nationalistic atmosphere in the Jewish schools. An ugly form of forcible Yiddishization took place where children who had studied for four years in a non-Jewish school, were transferred for their fifth year to the Yiddish-language school. M. Levitan condemned all these practices. But it must be pointed out that Levitan also stated that Yiddish-speaking children should only be educated in a Yiddish-language school, and that the graduates of the Yiddish school should be given an opportunity to continue their education in advanced schools (universities).

A special conference was also called by the Institute for Jewish Proletarian Culture of the Ukrainian Academy of Science, to discuss the position of Yiddish and the character of the language. This conference, held at the beginning of 1934, declared that both anti-Semitism and Jewish nationalism had been destroyed; that a system of Jewish education had been established, and that Yiddish was to be the language of administration and of the government apparatus. A literature, as well as a theater, which was national in form and socialist in content had been developed in Yiddish. The statement then quoted Stalin:

> The proletarian culture does not do away with national culture but it gives it content, and the national culture does not do away with proletarian culture, but it gives it form. The universal proletarian culture does not exclude, but it continues and feeds the national culture. Just as the national culture does not do away with, but it completes and enriches the universal proletarian culture.

After quoting Stalin, the statement declared that Yiddish had freed itself from most of the Hebrew words that came from the bourgeois, nationalist, clerical and nationalistic Jewish culture, which had been preserved and cultivated in Yiddish by the romantic Hebraists and Yiddishists. These Hebrew words and expressions would be replaced with adequate words. All expressions and words that were imbued with religious and national meaning, or were full of contempt for the toiling masses, were to be eliminated. The language would be enriched with internationalisms, words derived from Russian, Ukrainian and Belorussian. At the same time, the statement warned against introducing too many new foreign words, fearing "jargonization" of the language; it also warned against every attempt to ignore the specific nature of Yiddish, its construction, syntax, and idiomatic expressions.

The statement concluded with a quotation from Stalin's address at the sixteenth Party Conference, which suggested that, during the time of proletarian dictatorship, the national languages should be developed and allowed to bloom; at the same time conditions would be created when all national languages should be prepared for death and fusion in one universal language, and all national cultures in one universal socialist culture.[26]

Since the liquidation of the Jewish Sections of the Communist Party and the various local Jewish bureaus of the Communist Party, there were only "instructors" who watched for Communist "kashrut" of the schools. An atmosphere of denunciations, accusations, and incriminations surrounded the schools. Teachers and directors were accused of Yiddishism, nationalism, and petit-bourgeois tendencies. The stress upon culture as national in form only emptied the schools of all national Jewish content. Yiddish remained as the language of instruction, but it was purged of Jewish meaning as much as possible. Although Yiddish literature remained as a subject, it was taught from a distorted and Communistic point of view.

In the absence of national content, Yiddish was the only element that could save the Jews from total assimilation. The majority of Jews, however, were not Yiddishists, and because the Yiddish-language schools had been purged of all Jewishness, except for Yiddish in a de-Judaized form, the parents were not interested in sending their children there. The result was a general exodus from the Yiddish schools and a rush to enter Russian schools.

The Yiddish schools reached their nadir during the purges and trials of 1936–1938, when most of the Jewish Communists and functionaries were arrested and executed, including the chief instructor, M. Levitan, and the mighty editor of the Moscow daily, *Emes,* Moshe Litvakov. Hundreds of former members of the Jewish Sections of the Communist Party and education functionaries and important teachers were arrested with them.

No statistics about the Yiddish schools are available after 1935, but we can see that some schools were liquidated from reports in the surviving Yiddish press. The schools functioned until the German attack on Russia in June 1941.

The Moscow *Emes* of 1937 and 1938 reported the closing of some schools,[27] but it also called for preparing the schools for the new school year.[28] The *Emes* of July 9, 1938, announced that the Kalinindorf Yiddish Pedagogic Institute would accept applications for new students, all of whom must have passed an entrance examination in Yiddish and Yiddish literature. *Emes* of July 14, 1938, reported that nationalists had done a great deal of harm in the schools of the Kalinindorf region, but there were still 46 Yiddish schools. On July 17, 1938, the *Emes* reported that the Odessa Yiddish schools were preparing for the new school year, and that the Yiddish schools in Vinnitsa and Zelianpol were also being prepared for the new year. On July 30, 1938, *Emes* reported that the Vinnitsa Yiddish school, which had 400 children, needed a director. In the *Emes* of August 21, 1938, there were reports about Yiddish schools in Zhitomer and Bershad.

The *Emes* of June 22, 1938, reports about the general school system in Belorussia. There were also reports about Yiddish schools in Yeremayevke (June 21, 1938), Bielotserkov, Odessa, Uman (June 30, 1938), Shpoli (July 3, 1938); and the article stated that there were "many" Yiddish schools in the Ukraine (June 21, 1938). But the same newspaper reported that thirty students graduated from the Yiddish Section of the Odessa Pedagogical Institute; the Yiddish schools had only three openings and the graduates were advised to apply at Russian or Ukrainian schools (*Emes,* June 5, 1938).

The *Emes* reported the existence of Yiddish schools, giving special attention to the fact that in Bobroysk, Belorussia, the Yiddish school had 400 pupils, and a first class of 26 (July 8, 1938). At the same time it published the following article:

> The enemies of the people, the counter-revolutionary nationalists and Bundists, who for a long time carried on in the Kalinindorf Region, have done a great deal of damage in the school work. These counter-revolutionaries did not allow the organizing of Ukrainian-language schools, and those Ukrainian schools that existed were not provided with school materials and personnel. In the schools of the region the Russian language was ignored, and in many schools there were no teachers of Russian at all.[29]

Thus the *Emes* conducted a mild agitation for Yiddish schools and at the same time it discouraged the establishment of Ukrainian schools in the Jewish Kalinindorf region.[30]

Yakov Kantor, a Soviet Jewish writer and statistician who, fortunately, survived the purges, recently published a study about the Soviet census of 1959. This study appeared in the Yiddish *Bleter Far Geshikhte* that is published by the Jewish Historical Institute in Warsaw, Poland.[31] In the article, Yakov Kantor discussed the two processes going on now in Russia, the process of assimilation and the process of national consolidation. Each nationality in the Soviet Union had an institution which enabled it to retain its national identity. Kantor's concern was revealed in his remarks:

> Unfortunately the Jews [in Russia] belong to those national minorities where the factors to maintain and strengthen their culture have already been absent for a few decades, since the years of the strengthening of the personality cult. Under such conditions, the assimilationist tendencies get the upper hand.
>
> But one needs, and must, point out that even in the condition of the personality cult, there was no special policy towards the Jews. In the year 1938, together with the Jewish cultural institutions, all Polish, German, Lithuanian, Esthonian institutions, and also the institutions of those other national minorities that had any connection with the West were also liquidated. It was a result of the spy mania that, at that time, reached its culmination point.[32]

Yakov Kantor lived through that period and told about the liquidation of all the Jewish cultural institutions in 1938. No doubt many schools were closed down at that time by the local authorities, and perhaps most of the schools were closed down, but many schools survived until the outbreak of the German-Russian War in June 1941.

We have reports in the Kiev daily newspaper, *Der Shtern,* of Yiddish schools in 1939. In the issue of February 21, 1939, Professor Zaretsky reviews a new grammar by Khaim Loytsker and Shapiro. The same newspaper, issue of February 27, 1939, reported about the Yiddish school in Lubina. On June 15, 1939, *Der Shtern* announced that the Yiddish school for medical functionaries and technicians would accept applications, and that the applicants must pass examinations in Yiddish and Yiddish literature. The same issue of the *Shtern* contained the news that the Yiddish Pedagogical Institute of Dniepropetrovsk would accept applications, and a knowledge of Yiddish was required. There were also reports of Yiddish schools of Czenivke (January 4, 1939),

Vinnitsa (January 30, 1939), and Mezhibush (February 6, 1939). *Shtern* announced the organization of a committee to celebrate the eightieth birthday of Sholem Aleichem and called upon all Yiddish schools to participate (*Shtern*, January 4, 1939).

As late as 1941, on the eve of the outbreak of the Russo-German War, G. Yabrov wrote a new school guidebook called *Peretz far der Shul.* It was published in connection with the celebration of the ninetieth birthday of Y. L. Peretz by the Government Publishing House of Belorussia and the Commissariat of Education, Minsk, 1941 (42 pages). In the introduction G. Yabrov stated:

> According to our curriculum of Yiddish literature, Peretz is taught in the 6th and 9th grades. But in connection with his 90th birthday, Peretz should be taught this year in all grades, beginning with Grade V.
> Peretz's work should be taught as follows:
> Grade V—"The Seamstress," "The Moon Tells," "The Fast."
> Grade VI—"The Fast," "Three Seamstresses," "Married," "Wedding Dress."
> Grade VII—"Wedding Dress," "Married," "The Meshulach," "Death of a Musician."
> Grade VIII—"Death of a Musician," "In the Basement," "Bontche Shveig" (the Silent), "If Not Still Higher," "The Observant Cat," "Faith and Hope," "Brothers."
> Grade IX—*Monish,* "Shtrayml," "Observant Cat," "If Not Still Higher," "Between Two Mountains," some other poems.
> Grade X—*Monish,* "Shtrayml," "The Observant Cat," "If Not Still Higher," "Between Two Mountains," "Married," "Sholem Bais."

G. Yabrov also instructed the teachers to stress the biography of Peretz and discuss his work and accomplishments. At the end of the year a Peretz evening should be organized, with all classes participating in the assembly.

The guidebook clearly shows that Yiddish schools existed until the outbreak of the war; and that, although the Yiddish-language school had been purged of all nationalism, Yiddishism and most of its Jewish content, the children still read and studied such magnificent works as Peretz's "If Not Still Higher," and "Between Two Mountains."

Available evidence demonstrates that Yiddish schools existed in the Ukraine and Belorussia until June 1941, but it is also evident that the schools had declined since 1930. By 1939, the number of pupils attending Yiddish schools fell to about 75,000, which was only 20 percent of Jewish children of school age.[33] In retrospect, the reasons for the decline of the Yiddish schools are numerous and comprehensive. The liquidation of the Jewish Section of the Communist Party in 1930 left no organization to supervise normal development of the Yiddish schools; the fight against nationalism, against forcible Ukrainization and Belorussification, led to the opening of, and admittance of Jewish children to, the Russian-language schools; the struggle against Yiddishism, Jewish nationalism, led to the arrest and liquidations of teachers, "instructors," and personnel. Even during the best period of the Yiddish schools, the Jewish functionaries did not build any Yiddish universities, and thereby made it difficult for the graduates of the Yiddish schools to enter a general university. Parents and pupils thus preferred the Russian-language school, from which it was easier to enter a university. The almost complete de-Judaization of the Yiddish school, the elimination of most of the Hebrew elements from Yiddish, made many parents ask whether there was any difference in Jewishness between the Yiddish- and Russian-language schools. It is true that Yiddish still remained the language of instruction, but most of the parents were not Yiddishists, and they did not appreciate the value of Yiddish per se. Yiddish literature was taught from a Communist point of view. The pupils were acquainted with Yiddish classical writers, but this did not satisfy the parents who either wanted a full Jewish education, or none at all. The purges and the Moscow trials of 1936–1938 played havoc in the schools, and as Yakov Kantor stated, many schools were closed on account of the "spy mania."[34]

By 1939 the Yiddish schools reached a low point, although they existed until 1941. However, in September of 1939, a new life was infused in the Yiddish schools when the Soviet Army occupied the western parts of the Ukraine and Belorussia, which had previously belonged to Poland. Yiddish Communist schools were extended to the large Jewish population in that area. From September 17, 1939, until June 21, 1941, this western area became the center of Jewish cultural activity, which will be discussed in the final chapter.

A concluding emphasis must be placed upon the main reason for the decline of the Yiddish-language schools: Stalin's decision, founded upon Lenin's beliefs, to apply a program towards the Jews of total and forced assimilation. The liquidation of the schools was of prime importance in enforcing the "integration" of the Jews; for the Yiddish schools, though mostly de-Judaized, were still an important factor in maintaining Jewish consciousness and identity.

NOTES

1. *Emes,* Vol. 13, No. 57, March 9, 1930, Moscow.

2. *Bol'shaia Sovietskaia Entsiklopedia,* Vol. 24, p. 338, 1932.

3. Jacob Pat, *A Reyze* (A Trip), Warsaw, 1936, p. 253.

4. *Yidn in U.S.S.R.* (Jews in the Soviet Union), Moscow, 1935, p. 258.

5. Kh. Fialkov, *Vestnik Ope,* February 1914, St. Petersburg, quoted by Ch. Kazhdan, *Fun Kheyder un Shkoles Tsu Tsisho,* Mexico City, 1956, p. 138.

6. I. Dardak, "Unzere Dergreikhungen far 15 Yor Oktiaber afn Gebit fun Folk Bildung," in *Tsum XV Yortag fun der Oktiaber Revolutsie, Sotsial-Ekonomisher Zamlbukh,* Minsk, 1935, pp. 170–171.

7. Dardak, *op cit.,* pp. 165, 166.

8. *Ibid.,* p. 157.

9. Jacob Pat, *A Reyze* (A Trip), Warsaw, 1936, p. 248. In July–August, 1936, the present writer visited the Soviet Union and spent time in the city where he was born, Slutsk, and in Minsk and Kiev. To his amazement he saw how his uncles and cousins, whose language was Yiddish, spoke to their children and grandchildren in Russian. When asked, Why? they replied: "If we speak to them in Yiddish, the children will be sent, by local school authorities, to Yiddish-language schools, but if we talk to them in Russian, they can claim that their native language is Russian and they can enter a Russian-language school. There is more *takhles* in a Russian than in a Yiddish school, and it is more practical." By 1936, there were no more Jewish education functionaries to fight this tendency. Hence the decline of the Yiddish school.

10. M. Levitan, "Der Vuks fun Yidish Shprakhike Anshtaltn" (The Growth of Yiddish Language Institutions), *Ratn-Bildung,* No. 3, 1928, Kiev, pp. 3ff.

11. A. Kifer, *Ratn-Bildung,* no. 2, 1928, Kharkov, p. 3.

12. L. Mishkovsky, *Tsu di Sakhaklen fun II Alfarbundishn Kultur Tsuzamenfar* (The Balance of the II Cultural Conference), in *Ratn-Bildung,* No. 4, 1928, Kharkov.

13. M. Levitan, "Afn Shvel fun Zekhtsentn Yor" (On the Threshold of the Sixteenth Year), *Ratn-Bildung,* Nos. 10–12, 1932, Kiev, p. 52.

14. Gorokhov, "Di Shuln in Kamf far der Bashtimung fun Tsentral Komitet," in *Ratn-Bildung,* Nos. 7–8, July–August, 1932, p. 77.

15. *Ibid.*

16. Yakov Kantor, *Natsionalnaye Stroitelstvo Sredi Evryev S.S.S.R.* (National Construction Among the Jews in the U.S.S.R.), Moscow, 1934, pp. 173 ff.

17. Robert S. Sullivant, *Soviet Politics and the Ukraine,* New York, Columbia University Press, 1962, pp. 214, 215–216 ff. The present author reviewed Sullivant's book in *East Europe,* 1963.

18. Pat, *op. cit.,* p. 246.

19. Sullivant, *op. cit.,* p. 207.

20. *Kamf af Tsvei Frontn in der Pedagogie* (Struggle on two Fronts in Pedagogy), Government Publishing House for the National Minorities of the Ukraine, Kiev, Kharkov, 1932, p. 24.

21. *Ibid.*, p. 25.

22. *Ibid.*

23. *Kamf af Tsvei Frontn, ibid.*, p. 234.

24. A. Makagan, "Kegn yedn shpur fun Natsionalizm" (Against All Traces of Nationalism), *Ratn-Bildung*, Nos. 3–4, 1933, pp. 59 ff.

25. "Tsvang Yidishizatsie un Yidishizirer," *Ratn-Bildung*, No. 5, 1933, pp. 17–18.

26. *Ratn-Bildung*, No. 3, 1934, pp. 19–20.

27. *Emes*, June 24, 1937; Feb. 17, 1938.

28. *Emes*, August 26, 1938.

29. *Emes*, August 3, 1939.

30. The last issue of *Emes* appeared August 30, 1938. It was then suspended by the government.

31. *Bleter Far Geshikhte*, Vol. 15, 1962–1963, Warsaw. Yakov Kantor, "Einike Bamerkungen un Oysfirn tsu di Farefutlekhe Sakh'hakan fun der Folks Tseilung in *Ratn-Farband* dem 15th Yanuar, 1959" (Some Remarks and Conclusions about the Published Materials of the Census of the Soviet Union, the 15th of January, 1959).

32. *Ibid.*, p. 148. Kantor died recently in Moscow.

33. Jacob Lestschinsky, *Dos Sovetishe Yudentum* (Soviet Jewry), New York, 1941, p. 342.

34. See note 31.

CHAPTER 11

World War II, and the Final Liquidation of the Schools

ON September 17, 1939, Soviet Red armies crossed the Polish border, and within a few days occupied eastern Poland, the western parts of Belorussia and the Ukraine, where nearly 1,200,000 Jews were living. The Jews in this region lived a full and intensive Jewish life under Polish rule. Jewish education flourished and there were a great many Jewish schools of all types: Hebrew-secular, Hebrew-Orthodox, Yiddish, Polish Jewish and many yeshivot, among them Mir, Radin, Slomin, etc.[1]

Jewish functionaries from Minsk and Kiev were sent down to the newly acquired territories to sovietize Jewish cultural life. The government eliminated Polish and permitted the regions to be Ukrainized or Belorussified. The government policy could not allow Yiddish to be ignored, for it was the language of the Jews in that region.

The old Jewish-school system, with its hadorim, Hebrew and Yiddish schools, and yeshivot, was demolished by the government. Most of the schools were converted into Soviet Yiddish schools patterned after the Yiddish schools in the Soviet Union. Books were shipped from Moscow, Kiev, and Minsk.[2]

At the beginning of the Soviet occupation, a few Jewish educators hoped that the government would permit the existence of the Hebrew secular schools, in a sovietized form.[3] But a newly appointed Jewish functionary declared: "The Communist Party does not hate any language, and it does not hate Hebrew. If the Jewish masses spoke Hebrew, we would have Hebrew in the schools." But since the Jewish masses did not speak Hebrew, there was no need for Hebrew in the schools.[4]

The functionaries organized meetings at which both the parents and the teachers demanded the conversion of all previously existing Jewish schools into Soviet Yiddish-language schools.[5] Although the Ukrainians and Belorussians made some difficulties for the Yiddish schools, the Yiddish-language schools functioned and developed. Dr. Weinryb estimates that about one-third of the Jewish children of school age attended these Yiddish-language schools,[6] a good percentage considering that in the "original" Soviet Union only 20 percent of the Jewish children of school age attended Jewish schools at that period.

In June 1940, the Soviet armies occupied the three Baltic republics, Lithuania, Latvia, and Esthonia. The same process took place there. All religious and Hebrew schools were closed down and Soviet Yiddish schools opened.[7]

Because the Soviet government was interested in gaining the sympathy of the newly acquired population, it was not as harsh as in the "original" Soviet Union. Thus Yiddish dailies appeared in Vilna, Kaunas, Bialystok, and Lvov. Yiddish state theaters were opened, and Soviet Yiddish writers visited the new territories (Western Belorussia and Western Ukraine). The Yiddish schools were given full support and included in the regular school system.[8]

On June 21, 1941, the German Army attacked Russia, and within a short time all of Belorussia and the Ukraine were occupied. The Germans applied their systematic program of annihilating the entire Jewish population in that vast region. Before massacring the Jews, all Jewish institutions, including the schools, were automatically closed.

During the war years and the occupation of vast parts of the Soviet Union, a few Yiddish-language schools existed only in Birobidzhan. We have a report about the graduates of the Yiddish ten-year school in Birobidzhan who, upon their graduation in 1942, enlisted in the Soviet Army.[9] In 1944, the Yiddish schools in

Birobidzhan expanded, and Yiddish was introduced as a subject of study in the Russian-language schools.[10]

The Germans were driven out of the Soviet Union in 1944 and, upon the return of the Soviet government, the Jews who survived the occupation began to rebuild their lives. When it came to the problem of reestablishing the educational system, the government decided not to reopen the Yiddish schools.

In Vilna, or Vilnius, as the capital of Lithuania is now called, some Jewish writers and cultural functionaries, after great difficulty, received permission to open a four-year Yiddish school. When the school budget was submitted to the board of education at the end of the year, the provision that a fifth grade should be opened was refused by the school authorities. The authorities reasoned that those children who completed the first four grades of the Yiddish school knew sufficient Russian or Lithuanian to enter the fifth grade of a Russian or Lithuanian school. No permit to open a fifth grade meant the strangulation of the school.[11] One four-year Yiddish school was also permitted in Kaunas, the former capital of Lithuania, where Helena Khatskeles, the well-known pedagogue, was appointed director.[12]

The postwar years of 1945–1948 saw the final disappearance of the once flourishing Yiddish-school system. The two schools in Vilnius and Kaunas, and a few schools in the so-called Jewish autonomous region of Birobidzhan, plus the teachers' seminary and the school for medical personnel in the same "Jewish territory" were the last Jewish schools in Russia.

In November, 1948, the Soviet government apparently decided, once for all, to destroy the Jewish nationality. The only surviving Jewish organization, the Moscow Jewish Anti-Fascist Committee, was liquidated; all its members, with the exception of Ilya Ehrenburg, were arrested. The only Yiddish newspaper, the Moscow *Einikait*, was suspended. The only publishing house, Farlag Emes, was closed, and all Yiddish theaters were shut down at the same time as the few remaining Yiddish schools in Vilnius, Kaunas and Birobidzhan. Only the Birobidzhan Yiddish daily, *Shtern,* was permitted to continue publication as a three-day-a-week two-page publication, and at that it was merely a translation of the regional Russian daily. The circulation of the Birobidzhan *Shtern,* limited to that region alone, was only a thousand.

Thus, by 1948, were the last remnants of Jewish cultural life in Russia extinguished. Stalin carried out his brutal program of assimilating the Jews according to the principles of the Communist program that Lenin worked out in 1903–1906, and which he, in 1913, had set down in his brochure, "Marxism and the National Colonial Question."

Although the former ruler of Russia, Nikita Khrushchev, introduced a more liberal course, he maintained Stalin's policy towards the Jews. After many protests, he allowed the publication of a Yiddish bimonthly, *Sovietish Heimland,* the publication of a few books, and the presentation of Jewish concerts.[13] Considering the conditions imposed upon Soviet citizens, it is not surprising that no proposals were made to reestablish the Yiddish schools. However, in *Sovietish Heimland,*[14] a foreign Communist sympathizer suggested to the editor, Aaron Vergelis, the establishment of Yiddish afternoon supplementary schools. The editor, who is now the official spokesman of the Soviet government, replied: "The mothers of the children should want it first." But until the Soviet government wants it the mothers and fathers will not voice their desires. The Soviet government is still against the reestablishment of Yiddish schools, although outside pressure may influence the reestablishment of some schools.

The Soviet Jewish writer Yakov Kantor, in his essay in the *Jewish Historical Journal of Warsaw* quoted earlier,[15] challenged the Soviet census of 1959 and maintained that more than 20 percent of the Soviet Jews speak Yiddish. He thought that the percentage was so small because the question was phrased to confuse the people about *"Rodnoy Yazik"*—"native tongue." There are still reservoirs of Jewishness in the Soviet Union and, someday, a revival may take place, though we do not know in what form that revival will be expressed.

NOTES

1. Bernard D. Weinryb, "Polish Jews Under Soviet Rule," in *The Jews in the Soviet Satellites,* by Peter Meyer, Bernard D. Weinryb, Eugene Duschinsky, Nicholas Sylvan (Syracuse, 1953), pp. 332–333. Miriam Einstein, *Jewish Schools in Poland, 1919–1939,* New York, 1950.
2. Weinryb, *op. cit.,* p. 337.
3. Elkhanan Indelman, "Tarbut Be'Polin" ("Tarbut" in Poland), in Z. Scharfstein, editor, *Ha-Hinukh v'ha-Tarbut ha-Ivri be'Eropo bein Shtey Milchomoth*

ha'Olam (Hebrew Education and Culture in Europe Between the Two World Wars), New York, 1957, p. 133.

4. Beryl Kahan, "Ha-hinukh ha-Ivri be-Lita ha-atsmait" (Hebrew Education in Independent Lithuania), in Scharfstein, *op. cit.,* p. 168.

5. Kahan, *op. cit.,* p. 168.

6. Weinryb, *op. cit.,* p. 337.

7. Kahan, *op cit.,* pp. 168 ff.

8. Weinryb, *op. cit.,* pp. 336–337; Moshe Grossman, *In Farkisheftn Land fun Legendarishn Djugashvili* (In the Enchanted Land of Legendary Djugashvili), Vol. I, Paris, 1948, pp. 40 ff.

9. *Einikait,* September 15, 1942, Moscow.

10. I. Nusinov, *Einikait,* November 8, 1944, Moscow.

11. S. Kaczerginski, *Tsvishn Hamer un Serp* (Between Hammer and Sickle), Paris, 1949, p. 47.

12. *Einikait,* December 21, 1944, October 9, 1945, Moscow.

13. The *Sovetish Heimland* of July–August, 1964, carried the announcement that beginning with January, 1965, it would be converted into a monthly, which in fact happened.

14. *Sovetish Heimland,* No. 3, May–June, 1964, Moscow.

15. See note 31, Chapter X.

Some Conclusions
and Perspectives

ONLY half a century ago, Russian Jewry constituted the most important and creative part of world Jewry. The Jewish community of Tsarist Russia, which embraced a great part of Poland and the Baltic states, was a steaming hive of variegated activity. The Jews who lived in Jewish towns *(shtetlech)* and in Jewish quarters of large cities in the restricted Pale of Settlement had developed their own institutions and their own way of life which were uniquely and extensively Jewish. Every town and city had its synagogues and various Jewish schools as well as many institutions, organizations, and mutual self-aid societies. Jewish literature in Hebrew and Yiddish flourished—and there were also Jewish writers who wrote in Russian about Jews and Jewish problems. There was a trilingual Jewish press in Hebrew, Yiddish, and Russian, and many publishing houses that published all types of Jewish books in the three languages. On the eve of the first World War, Russia was the center of both Hebrew and Yiddish literatures.

The first World War and the Bolshevik coup of November 1917 completely changed the picture of Russian Jewry. Although Poland and the three Baltic republics became independent, three million Jews still remained in the Soviet Union. Between 1918 and

1936 the government permitted Jewish cultural and educatiònal activity, a system of Yiddish schools was established, Yiddish newspapers, magazines and books were published, and there were even a few research institutions that engaged in Jewish research. There were also a number of Jewish theaters and singing societies.

By the mid-thirties official policy had changed. Some of the cultural institutions began to disappear and the government began to liquidate Yiddish schools and various research institutions. The Kiev Institute for Jewish Proletarian Culture, for example, was closed by the government in May 1936. Even before that, there had been a decline of Jewish cultural activity due to a tendency of Soviet Jewry to assimilate or acculturate. By that time, many young Jews had adopted Russian as their language, but no Jewish institutions using the Russian language were permitted. Jewish cultural activity, in a limited form, was carried on during the prewar years. It was revived in the newly occupied territories in 1939–1941. Yiddish schools, daily newspapers, and state theaters were founded in the former Polish territories and in the Baltic states.

During the Soviet-German War, 1941–1945, all the newly acquired territories and the areas of Russia where the majority of the Jewish population lived, were occupied by the Germans in the first few months of the war. Of the five million Jews who lived in the Soviet Union in June 1941, it is estimated that more than two million perished at the hands of the Germans. All the Yiddish schools and cultural institutions were destroyed by the Nazis. Only a small weekly newspaper and a few books were published during the war in Moscow. In Birobidzhan a few schools functioned, and a small newspaper was published, but it was distributed in that region only.

After the war there was a slight revival, but under Stalin's directives all remaining Jewish institutions, including the Moscow Jewish Anti-Fascist Committee, were shut down, and most of the functionaries, including the most important Yiddish writers, were arrested. All this occurred in November 1948. In August 1952 thirty Yiddish writers were executed and hundreds perished in various concentration camps.

After Stalin's death, in 1953, the surviving Yiddish writers were released and rehabilitated. Due to world public opinion and pressure, the government permitted a slight easing of the restrictions on Jewish cultural activity. Concerts of Yiddish songs were allowed, six books in Yiddish were published and a Yiddish bimonthly, *Sovietish Heimland,* was launched in Moscow.[1]

At the present time there are no Yiddish schools in the Soviet Union, not even in the so-called Jewish autonomous region in Birobidzhan. There are no Jewish cultural institutions, nor Jewish organizations. A Hebrew-Russian dictionary was published in Moscow in 1963. However, as far as can be ascertained, Hebrew and ancient Jewish history are taught only in a few universities, but these courses are open only to a limited number of students who specialize in archaeology and philology. It is apparent that the Soviet government is trying to assimilate the Russian Jews. Such minorities as the Germans and the Poles, who are not concentrated in any territory, have various cultural institutions through which they can perpetuate their language and culture. No such opportunity is given the Jews.[2]

From observation and study it is obvious that a great many Jews long for Jewish identification and for Jewish culture. The Jewish concerts are attended by a great many people. An American Jewish writer and communal worker who visited Russia, reported on the enthusiasm of a Jewish audience at a Jewish concert in Moscow.[3]

The Moscow Jewish journal *Sovietish Heimland* which now appears monthly is, within the limitations sanctioned by the authorities, a Jewish journal that publishes stories, novels, poems, about Jews and Jewish life.[4] The editorial office of this journal is becoming an unofficial center for Jewish activities. Visitors are received there and discussions with the editor, A. Vergelis, have become a common occurrence.[5] The journal arranged a number of literary evenings in Moscow, Vilnius, Kiev, Odessa, where Jewish writers read stories and poems and were acclaimed by large audiences.

Recently a conference was held at the editorial offices of the journal, which was attended by a number of Yiddish writers from Moscow, Leningrad, Kiev, Riga, Czernowitz, Kursk, Kazan, and Kharkov. Officially this was a conference about literary research, but the conference also discussed the possibilities of launching another journal and the publication of a text book for teaching Yiddish.

It was also announced at the conference that a Yiddish-Russian dictionary, which was prepared before the second World War and was presumed lost, was recently discovered and would be published in Moscow in 1965.[6]

From all these facts it is obvious Soviet Jewry would welcome the relaxation of government restrictions on Yiddish cultural activities. The possible revival of the Yiddish-school system is a complicated matter. We have already quoted A. Vergelis' answer to an inquiry about the possibility of reopening the Yiddish schools (pp. 258–259). Vergelis said that the "mothers should want it first." However, it is primarily not a question of the mothers wanting it, but of the readiness of the government to authorize it. Naturally, the interest of the mothers is also important.

Most of the Jewish population of the U.S.S.R. is now more widely dispersed in the country than in the past. It is doubtful whether the parents who live in Moscow, Leningrad, Kiev, Kazan, or Kursk would send their children to a Yiddish day school. However, there is no doubt that there would be some parents in Vilnius, Kaunas, Czernowitz, and in some towns in the Ukraine as well as in Birobidzhan who would be willing to do so, provided that no discriminations were practiced against the graduates of such schools when they applied to universities or technical schools. There is also no question of the willingness of many parents to send their children to an afternoon Jewish school.

It must be emphasized that the Jews could not expect any privileges and, since Soviet law prohibits the teaching of religion to school children, these schools would have to be secular. The old Soviet ban on teaching Hebrew is still in effect (it is being taught now, as previously mentioned, at a few universities as part of courses in archaeology and philology). The introduction to the Hebrew-Russian dictionary states that Hebrew is now the language of Israel;[7] this might be some indication that the ban on teaching Hebrew would be lifted. This is unlikely, however, for the very reason that Hebrew is associated with Israel. The schools, therefore, if they were reopened, whether they were all day, or supplementary, would be Yiddish-language schools, with the emphasis on Yiddish literature and Jewish history, taught from a Marxist point of view. If, under pressure, the Soviet government allowed a partial revival of Yiddish cultural activity, it may, under more and constant pressure from the Western world, allow the establishment of a few day or afternoon schools. Under the Soviet regime the most that we can expect in the field of Jewish education is the type of Yiddish school that existed prior to 1948. This would be a Soviet school in Yiddish, with Yiddish and Yiddish literature as part of the curriculum.

It is my belief, from studying the problem, that the graduates of the Yiddish schools not only knew Yiddish and Yiddish literature, and a little of Jewish history, but they felt their Jewishness more than the Jewish children who did not attend the Yiddish schools. The studying of Yiddish and Yiddish literature had a nationalizing effect.

A revival of Jewishness in the Soviet Union is impossible without the reestablishment of some form of Jewish education. Jewish education in the Soviet Union will reemerge only as the result of the exertion of pressure by world Jewry.

NOTES

1. As of 1970 about twenty-seven titles have been published.
2. Maurice Friedberg, "The State of Soviet Jewry," *Commentary,* January 1965, pp. 38–43.
3. I. Zelitch, "Der Klang fun Yidishe Lider in Moskve" (The Sound of Yiddish Songs in Moscow), *Oifn Shvel* (New York, October 1964), pp. 6–7.
4. Elias Schulman, "Sovietish Heimland: Lone Voices, Stifled Creators," *Judaism,* Winter 1965, New York.
5. L. Levi, "Pegisha im Aharon Vergelis" (A Meeting with Aaron Vergelis), *Ha-Aretz,* Tel Aviv, January 22, 1965, pp. 10–13.
6. P. Novick, "Tif Zainen di Vortslen" (Deep Are the Roots), *Morgn Freiheit,* New York, January 10, 1965, p. 5. It has not been published yet (1970).
7. *Ivrit-Russki Slovar* (Hebrew-Russian Dictionary), compiled by F. L. Shapiro, edited by Professor B. M. Grande, Government Publishing House for Foreign and International Dictionaries, Moscow, 1963, p. 4.

Bibliography

*Only items referred to in
the text or in footnotes or
of direct relevance to the
study are included.*

Abraham, L., Knikhon, I., Kaplan, K. *Der Mishpet Ibern Kheyder* (The Trial of the Heder). Vitebsk: 1922.
Agliad. (Catalogue of Courses, University of Minsk). Minsk: 1926.
Agurski, S. *Der Yidisher Arbeiter in der Komunistisher Bavegung 1917–1921* (The Jewish Worker in the Communist Movement). Minsk: 1925.
——————. *Di Oktiaber Revolutsie in Vaysrusland* (The October Revolution in Belorussia). Minsk: 1927.
——————, Osherowitch, A., Frishman, W., and Spenser, B. (editors). *Lenin Kegn Bund* (Lenin Against the Bund). Minsk: 1935.
Aksenfeld, Israel. *Verk* (Works). Edited by Meyer Winer. Kiev: 1931.
Aleksandrove, E., and Bensman, T. *Ershte Trit* (First Steps). Minsk: 1932.
A Yor Arbet fun der R.K.P. in der Yidisher Svive (A Year's Work of the Russian Communist Party in the Jewish Environment). Moscow: 1924.
Baron, Salo W. *The Russian Jew Under Tsars and Soviets.* New York: 1964.
Becker, Joseph. "Folks Shprakhn un Folks Shuln" (Folk Languages and Public Schools), *Folkstsaitung* Nos. 18, 21, 24, 27. Vilna: March 1906.
——————. "Konferents fun Mefitse Haskalah" (Conference of Mefitse Haskalah) in *Tsum Moment.* Petrograd: February 1916.
Berkman and Lerner. *Tal Boker* (Morning Dew). Warsaw: 1908.
Bolshaya Sovietskaya Entsiklopediya, Vol. 24. Moscow: 1932.
Brakhman, A. "Di Bolshevistishe Partei in Kamf far der Leizung fun der Yidnfrage" (The Bolshevik Party in the Struggle to Solve the Jewish Problem) in *Forpost,* No. 1. Birobidzhan: 1936, pp. 130–148.

――――――. "Der Kamf fun Leninen un Stalinen Kegn Yidishn Natsionalizm" (The Struggle of Lenin and Stalin against Jewish Nationalism) in *Forpost* No. 2. Birobidzhan: 1936.

Bukhbinder N., Greenberg, Z., Dimanshtein, S. *Kultur Fragn* (An Almanac), Vol. I. Petrograd: 1918.

Burganski, P. *Leienbukh* (A Reader). Kiev: 1936.

――――――. *Zai Greyt* (Be Prepared). Kiev: 1932.

Counts, George S. *The Challenge of Soviet Education.* New York: 1957, pp. 60–61, 82–95.

Dardak, I. "Unzere Dergreikhungen far 15 Yor Oktiaber afn Gebit fun Folk Bildung" (Our Achievement for 15 Years of the October Revolution in the Field of Public Education) in *Tsum XV Yortag fun der Oktiaber Revolutsie* (On the XV Anniversary of the October Revolution). Minsk: 1932.

Der Nayer Veg (The New Road), No. I. Vilna: 1906.

Di Bashtimung fun C.C.K.P.B. Vegn der Onfang un Mitlshul (The Decisions of the Central Committee of the All-Union Communist Party-Bolsheviks about the Elementary and Secondary School). Minsk: 1931.

Di Ershte Yidishe Shprakh Konferents 1908 (The First Yiddish Language Conference). Vilna: 1931.

Dimanshtein, S. *Baym Likht Fun Komunism* (By the Light of Communism). Moscow: 1919.

―――――― (ed.). "Kultur Boyung Tsvishn di Yidishe Masn" (Cultural Construction Among the Jewish Masses) in *Yidn in F.S.S.R.* (Jews in the U.S.S.R.). Moscow: 1935, pp. 257–267.

Dos Naye Lebn (The New Life). Petrograd: 1916.

Dubnov, S. *Divrei Yeme Am Olam* (World History of the Jewish People), Vol. XI. Tel Aviv: 1940.

Eisenstein, Miriam. *Jewish Schools in Poland 1919–1939.* New York: 1950.

Erik, Max. *Di Komedies fun der Berliner Oyfklerung* (The Comedies of the Berlin Enlightenment). Kiev: 1933.

――――――, and Rozenzweig, A. *Di Yidishe Literatur in XIX Yorhundert* (Yiddish Literature in the Nineteenth Century). Kiev: 1935.

Etinger, Shlomo. *Geklibene Verk* (Selected Works). Edited by Max Erik. Kiev: 1935.

Evreiskaia Entsiklopediya (Jewish Encyclopedia), Vol. XV, Column 593. St. Petersburg: 1910.

Evreiskaia Vesti (Jewish News). Moscow: 1917.

Evreiskaia Zhizn (Jewish Life), No. 18. Moscow: November 1, 1915.

Falkowitch, E. *Yidish* (Yiddish). Moscow: 1936.

Fialkov, Khaim. *Folks Ertsiung* (Public Education). Petrograd: 1918.

Folksbildung (Public Education). Vilna: 1919.

Friedberg, Maurice. "The State of Soviet Jewry," *Commentary.* New York: January 1965.

Frumkin, Maria Yakovlevna (Esther). "Einike Bamerkungen Vegn Natsionaler Dertsiung" (A Few Remarks About National Education). *Tsait Fragn*, No. 1, Vilna: 1909; and *Tsait Fragn*, No. 5, Vilna: 1911.

——————. "Vegn di Nontste Oyfgobn un dem Inhalt fun der Arbet fun di Yidsektsies" (About the Immediate Problems and the Content of the Work of the Jewish Sections) in *A Yor Arbet fun der R.K.P. in der Yidisher Svive* (A Year's Work of the Russian Communist Party in the Jewish Environment). Moscow: 1924.

——————. *Tsu der Frage fun der Yidisher Folkshul* (The Problem of the Jewish Public Schol). Vilna: 1910. Petrograd: 1917.

Fun Tog Tsu Tog (From Day to Day). Petrograd: February 1916.

Genrikh, S. "Di Kultur Oiftuen fun der Ruslendisher Ratn Republic" (The Cultural Accomplishments of the Russian Soviet Republic) in *Di Naye Velt* (The New World), Nos. 1–2 (combined issue). Vilna: 1919.

Gergel, N. "Di Pogromen in Ukraine in di Yorn 1918–1921" (The Pogroms in the Ukraine in the Years 1918–1921), in *Yivo Shriftn far Ekonomik* (Yivo Studies in Economics), Vol. I. Vilna: 1928.

Gilinsky, S. "Tsu der Geshikhte fun Yidishn Shulvezn in Varshe" (On the History of the Yiddish-School System in Warsaw), *Shul un Lebn* (School and Life). Warsaw: January, 1922.

Golomb, Abraham. "Di Yidish Veltlekhe Shul" (The Yiddish Secular School) in *Shul Almanakh* (School Almanac). Philadelphia: 1935.

——————. *A Halber Yorhundert Yidishe Dertsiung* (Half a Century of Jewish Education). Rio de Janeiro: 1957.

Gorokhov, G. "Di Shuln in Kamf far der Bashtimung fun Tsentral Komitet" (The Schools in the Struggle for the Decisions of the Central Committee) in *Ratn Bildung* (Soviet Education), Nos. 7–8 (combined issue). Kiev: 1932.

——————. *Lenin Vegn Fragn fun Pedagogie un Shul Boyung* (Lenin about Problems of Pedagogy and School Development). Kiev: 1934.

Greenbaum, Abraham. *Jewish Scholarship in Soviet Russia 1918–1941.* (Mimeographed.) Boston: 1959.

Greenberg, I., and Greenberg, M. *Yidn Af Erd* (Jews on Soil). Moscow: 1930.

Groser, P. K. *Nighlizma Dzhana Dewey* (The Nihilism of John Dewey). Moscow: 1958.

Heifetz, Elias. *The Slaughter of the Jews in the Ukraine in 1919.* New York: 1921.

Hokhberg, David. *Di Naye Shul* (The New School). Vilna: 1914.

Holdes, A., Shames, P. *Literarishe Khrestomatie* (Literary Chrestomathy). Kiev: 1934.

Holmshtok, Kh., Mishkovsky, L., Rives, S., Bakst, I., and Shulman, N. *Oktiaber Kinder* (October Children). Moscow: 1926.

Horowitz, H. D. "Fun Kheydesh tsu Kheydesh" (From Month to Month), *Di Yidishe Velt.* Vilna: July 1913.

Hurwitz-Zalkes, S. *Amol iz Geven* (Once Upon a Time). New York: 1950.

Indelman, Elkhanan. "Tarbut Be'Polin" (Tarbut in Poland) in Zevi Scharfstein, editor, *Ha-Hinukh ve'ha-Tarbut ha'Ivri Be'Eropo Bein Shtey Milkhomoth Ha'Olam* (Hebrew Education and Culture in Europe Between the Two World Wars). New York: 1957.

Istoria Sovetskoi Konstituti i Dekretakh (History of the Soviet Constitution and Decrees). Moscow: 1936.

Kaczerginski, S. *Tsvishn Hamer un Serp* (Between the Hammer and Sickle). Paris: 1949.

Kahan, Beryl. "Ha-Hinukh Ha-ivri Be-Lita Ha-Atsmait" (Hebrew Education in Independent Lithuania) in Zevi Scharfstein, editor, *Ha-Hinukh ve'ha-Tarbut ha'Ivri Be'Eropo Bein Shtey Milkhomoth Ha'Olam* (Hebrew Education and Culture in Europe Between the Two World Wars). New York: 1957.

Kalinin, Mikhail I. "Vegn der Yidisher Autonomer Gegnt" (About the Jewish Autonomous Region) in *Yidn in F.S.S.R.* (Jews in the U.S.S.R.). Moscow: 1936.

Kamf af Tsvei Frontn in der Pedagogie (Struggle on Two Fronts in Pedagogy). Kiev-Kharkov: 1932.

Kantor, Yakov. "Di Kultur Revolutsie in der Yidisher Svive" (The Cultural Revolution in the Jewish Environment), *Ratn-Bildung* (Soviet Education) No. 4; Kharkov: May 1928.

――――――. "Einike Bamerkungen un Oysfirn tsu di Farefentlikhe Sakhhaklen fun der Folks Tseilung in Ratn-Farband dem 15 Yanuar, 1959 (Some Remarks and Conclusions About the Published Materials of the Census of the Soviet Union, the 15th of January 1959) in *Bleter far Geshikhte* (Historical Leaves), Vol. 15. Warsaw: 1962–1963.

――――――. *Di Yidishe Bafelkerung in Ukraine* (The Jewish Population in the Ukraine). Kiev: 1929.

――――――. *Natsionalnoe Stroitelstvo Sredi Yevreiev F.S.S.R.* (National Construction Among the Jews in the U.S.S.R.). Moscow: 1934.

Karun, A. "Ha'Kursim ha'Pedagogiim Be'Grodno" (The Hebrew Pedagogical Courses in Grodno) in *Rishonim*, edited by M. A. Baigel, I. Man, and I. Rubin, Tel Aviv: 5696.

Kautsky, Karl. *Are the Jews a Race?* Translated from the Second German Edition. London: 1926.

Kazhdan, Khaim S. *Fun Kheyder un Shkoles tso Tsisho* (From Heder and Schools to Tsisho). Mexico City: 1956.

Kilpatrick, William Heard. *Philosophy of Education.* New York: 1951.

Kline, George L., editor. "Pavlov's Teachers' Training Schools" in *Soviet Education*, pp. 121 ff. London: 1957.

Klitenik, S. *Kultur Arbet Tsvishn di Yidishe Arbetndike inem Ratn-Farband* (Cultural Work Among the Jewish Toilers in the Soviet Union). Moscow: 1931.

Kopelev, F. F. *Sovietskaia Shkola v'Period Sotsialisticheskoy Industrializatsia* (The Soviet School in the Period of Socialist Industrialization). Moscow: 1951.

Lenin, V. I. *Sochineniya* (Works), Volumes VI, XVI, XVII, XVIII, 2nd edition. Moscow: 1928.

Lestschinsky, Jacob. *Dos Sovetishe Yudentum* (Soviet Jewry). New York: 1941.

————. "Di Yidishe Shtudirnde Yugnt" (The Jewish Student Youth) in *Di Yidishe Velt* (The Jewish World) No. 5 and No. 6. Vilna: May 1914 and June 1914.

Levi, L. "Pegisha im Aharon Vergelis" (A Meeting with Aaron Vergelis) in *Ha'Aretz*. Tel-Aviv: January 22, 1965.

Levine, Yacov, Lukowsky I., and Hurwitz, S. *Unzer Naye Shul* (Our New School). A Reader for the Second and Third Years. Warsaw: 1914.

Levinson, Boris. "Di Yidishe Folkshul" (The Yiddish Public School), in *Di Naye Tsait*, No. 1. Vilna: 1908.

————. "Vegn Natsionaler Dertsiung" (About National Education) in *Tsait-Fragn*, No. 3. Vilna: March 1910.

Levitan, M. "Afn Shvel fun Zekhtsentn Yor" (On the Threshold of the Sixteenth Year), *Ratn-Bildung*, Nos. 10-12 (combined issue). Kiev: 1932.

————. "Der Vuks fun Yidish Shprakhike Anshtaltn" (The Growth of Yiddish-Language Institutions), *Ratn-Bildung*, No. 3. Kiev: 1928.

————. "Vegn Kultur Arbet" (About Cultural Work), *A Yor Arbet fun der R.K.P. in der Yidisher Svive* (A Year's Work of the Russian Communist Party in the Jewish Environment). Moscow: 1924.

————. "Tsvang Yidishizatsie un Yidishizirer" (Forcible Yiddishization and Yiddishizers), *Ratn-Bildung*, No. 5. Kiev: 1933.

Litvakov, Moishe. "Dos Sovetishe Yidishe Folk" (The Soviet Jewish Nation), *Emes*. Moscow: November 7, 1936.

Loytsker, Khaim, and Shapiro, M. *Gramatik* (Grammar), Part I, Morphology for V and VI Grades. Kiev: 1940.

Makagan, A. "Kegn Edn Shpur fun Natsionalizm" (Against All Traces of Nationalism), *Ratn-Bildung*, Nos. 3-4 (combined issue). Kiev: 1933.

————. Mishkovsky, L., and Spivack, Eliahu. *In Kamf* (In the Struggle). Kharkov: 1930.

Marek, Peter S. *Ocherki po Istorii Prosveschenia Evrev Rossi* (Studies in the History of Jewish Enlightenment in Russia). Moscow: 1909.

Mishkovsky, L. "Tsu di Sakh'aklen fun II Alfarbandishn Yidishn Kultur Tsuzamenfor" (The Balance of the II All-Union Yiddish Cultural Conference), *Ratn-Bildung*, No. 4, pp. 2–6. Kiev: 1928.

Mishkovsky, Noah. "Di Ershte Yidishe Veltlekhe Shuln in Russland" (First Yiddish Secular Schools in Russia), in *Shul Almanakh*. Philadelphia: 1935.

————. *Mein Lebn un Meine Raizes* (My Life and Travels), Vol. I. Mexico City: 1947.

Myerson, I. *Unzer Geshikhte, fun dem Onheib Bizn Hurbn fun Bais Sheiny* (Our History from the Beginning to the Destruction of the Second Temple). Kiev: 1912.

Niger, S. (S. Charney). "Di Vispe" (The Island), *Dos Naye Lebn*. Petrograd: 1916.

————. *In Kamf far a Nayer Dertsiung* (In the Struggle for a New Education). New York: 1940.

Nikolski, N. M. *Dos Uralte Folk Isroel* (Ancient Israel). Yiddish by A. Rosenthal. Moscow: 1919–1920.

——————. *Geshikhte—Di Farklasindike Gezelshaft, der Uralter Mizrakh, di Antike Velt* (History—the Pre-class Society, the Ancient East, the Ancient World), translated by Uri Finkel. Moscow: 1934.

——————. *Yidishe Yomteyvim, Zeyer Oyfkum un Antviklung* (Jewish Holidays, Their Origin and Development). Minsk: 1935.

Novick, P. "Tif Zainen di Vertlen" (Deep Are the Roots), in *Morgn Freiheit*. New York: January 10, 1965.

Olgin, M. *Dos Yidishe Vort* (The Yiddish Word). Vilna: 1912.

Oyslender, Nahum. *Leienbukh* (A Reader) For 2nd and 3rd Years. Kiev: 1936.

——————, Volkenshtein, D., Lurie, N., Fininberg, Ezra. *Yidishe Literatur* (Yiddish Literature), Part I. Kiev: 1928.

Pat, Jacob. *A Rayze* (A Trip). Warsaw: 1936.

Pilch, Judah. *The Heder Methukhan*. Unpublished dissertation, Dropsie College, Philadelphia, Pa., 1952.

Program fun Yidish Literatur I–VII (Curriculum for Yiddish and Yiddish Literature). Minsk: 1925.

Program fun Yidish un Literatur far der Zibnyoriker Shul (Curriculum for Yiddish and Literature for the Seven-Year School). Minsk: 1927.

Pupko, Chaim. "Vilna, dos Vigele fun der Yidisher Veltlekher Shul" (Vilna, Cradle of the Yiddish Secular School). *In Vilna*, edited by Y. Yeshurin. New York: 1935.

Raphaeli, Arya (Tsentsiper). *Esser Sh'enot Redifot* (Ten Years of Persecution). Tel Aviv: 1930.

——————. *Be'Maavak Le'Geulah* (In the Struggle for Redemption). Tel Aviv: 1956.

Ravin, I., Shatz, V. *Literatur* (Literature) for the IV Year. Minsk: 1933.

Reisen, Abraham. "Di Ershte Yidish-Veltlekhe Shul" (The First Yiddish Secular School) in *Unzer Shul* (Our School). New York: October 1932, pp. 7–9.

"Research Staff of the Commission on European Jewish Cultural Reconstruction; Tentative List of Jewish Educational Institutions in Axis Occupied Countries," *Jewish Social Studies*, Vol. VIII, No. 3. New York: July 1946.

Revutsky, A. *In di Shvere Teg af Ukraine* (In the Difficult Days in the Ukraine). Berlin: 1924.

Rezolutsjes Ukrainishe Konferents fun di Yidishe Sektsies fun der Komunistisher Partei (Resolutions of the All-Ukrainian Conference of the Jewish Sections of the Communist Party). Kiev: 1926.

Rubin, I., Khanutin, K., Holmshtok, K., Aleksandrov, H., and Dardak, I. *Gezelshaftkentenish* (Social Studies). Minsk: 1928.

Salgaller, Emanuel. "Anthropology in Miniature, a Note on the Jews of Soviet Georgia," in *Jewish Social Studies*, Vol. XXVI, No. 4. New York: October, 1964.

Schalit, Moishe. *Vilner Kulturele Anshtaltn* (Vilna Cultural Institutions). Vilna: 1916.

Scharfstein, Zevi. *Toledot Ha-Hinukh Be'Yisroel* (History of Jewish Education), Vol. I. New York: 1945.

—————. *Ha'Heder be Khayye Ameinu* (The Heder in the Life of Our People). New York: 1943.

Schulman, Elias. "Sovietish Heimland: Lone Voices, Stifled Creators," in *Judaism*, New York. Winter.: 1965.

Schwartz, Solomon M. *The Jews in the Soviet Union*. Syracuse: 1951.

Shapiro, F. L. *Ivrit-Russki Slovar* (Hebrew-Russian Dictionary), edited by Professor B. M. Grande. Moscow: 1963.

Shevkin, B. *Pedagogika Dzhana Dewey na Sluzhbe Sovremenoi Amerikanskoi Reaktsi* (The Pedagogy of John Dewey in Service of Contemporary American Reaction). Moscow: 1952.

Shpieryan, M. *Yidish, A Konspekt fun a Kurs in dem II Moskver Melukhishn Univerzitet* (Yiddish, A Syllabus of a Course in the II Moscow Government University). Moscow: 1926.

Shtern, Yekhiel. *Kheyder un Beys Medresh* (Heder and Beys Medresh, a Study in Traditional Jewish Education). New York: 1950.

Shtif, N. *Di Eltere Yidishe Literatur* (The Older Yiddish Literature). Kiev: 1929.

Skuratovsky, editor. *Gezelshaftkentenish* (Social Studies). Translated into Yiddish by A. Altchul, G. Gorokhov, A. Yuditsky, and I. Khunkhin. Kiev: 1930.

Spivack, Eliahu. *Arum Undz* (Around Us). Kiev: 1927.

—————. *Undzer Vort* (Our Word). Kiev: 1929.

—————. *Yidish* (Yiddish). Kiev: 1923.

—————. *Yidishe Shprakh* (Yiddish Language). Kiev: 1928.

Stalin, Josef. *Marksizm i Natsionalny Vopros* (Marxism and the National Question). Moscow: 1934.

Strashun, A., compiler. *Di Yidishe Autonomie un der Natsionaler Sekretariat in Ukraine, Materialn un Dokumentn* (The Jewish Autonomy and the National Secretariat in the Ukraine, Materials and Documents). Kiev: 1920.

Strizhak, L., and Buzevitch, A. "Konspekt far Lernen Yidishe Geshikhte" (Outline for Teaching Jewish History), in *Ratn-Bildung*, No. 3. Kiev: 1928.

Sullivant, Robert S. *Soviet Politics and the Ukraine*. New York: 1962.

Tcherikower, Eliahu. "Komunistishe Kemfer far Hebreish in Turkestan" (Communist Fighters for Hebrew in Turkestan), in *Der Tekufe fun Revolutsie* (In the Revolutionary Period), Vol. I. Berlin: 1924.

Tehemeriski, A. *Di Alfarbandishe Komunistishe Partey Bolshevikes un di Yidishe Masn* (The All Union Communist Party Bolsheviks and the Jewish Masses). Moscow: 1936.

Tsaitshrift, Vol. IV. Minsk: 1930.

Tsum XV Yortog fun der Oktiaber Revolutsie Zamlbukh (On the Fifteenth Anniversary of the October Revolution, an Almanac). Minsk: 1932.

Vestnik, Evreiskovo Prosveshchenia (Courier of Jewish Education). Petrograd: March 1916.

Visenshaftlekhe Yorbikher, Band I (Scientific Yearbooks—Vol. I). Moscow: 1929.

Weinryb, Bernard D. "Das Judishe Schulwesen in Sowjetrussland," (The Jewish School System in Soviet Russia), *Monatsschrift fur Geschichte und Wissenschaft des Judentums* (LXXV), Nos. 11–12, Nov.-Dec. 1931, pp. 455–462.

Winer, Meyer, editor. *Verk fun Isroel Aksenfeld* (Works of Israel Aksenfeld). Kiev: 1931.

Yabrov, G. *Literarishe Khrestomatie* (Literary Chrestomathy). Minsk: 1926.

—————. *Peretz far der Shul* (Peretz for the School). Minsk: 1941.

Yafe, Leib. *Der Shul Khaver* (The School Friend). Vilna: 1914.

Yedies—Partei-Materialn (News—Party Materials) of the Central Bureau of the Jewish sections of the Russian Communist Party. Moscow: 1921.

Yivo News, No. 83. New York: July 1962.

Zaretsky, Isaac. *Gramatick un Ortografie* (Grammar and Orthography). Kiev: 1934.

Zelitch, I. "Der Klang fun Yidishe Lider in Moskve" (The Sound of Yiddish Songs in Moscow), *Oifn Shvel.* New York: October 1964.

Zerva, A. "Bildungs Fragn" (Educational Problems), in *Dos Yidishe Vort* (The Yiddish Word), pp. 14–18. Petrograd: January 1916.

Zilberfarb, M. *Dos Yidishe Ministerium un di Yidishe Autonomie in Ukraine* (The Ministry of Jewish Affairs and Jewish Autonomy in the Ukraine). Kiev: 1918.

Index